MW00799845

LETTERS

AND

NUMBERS

FOR

NEEDLEPOINT

LETTERS
AND
NUMBERS
FOR
NEEDLEPOINT

E. M. Parker

CHARLES SCRIBNER'S SONS   •   NEW YORK

Copyright © 1978 Elinor Parker

Library of Congress Cataloging in Publication Data

Parker, Elinor Milnor, 1906-
    Letters and numbers for needlepoint.

    1. Canvas embroidery—Patterns.   2. Alphabets.
3. Numerals.   I. Title.
TT778.C3P36   746.4'4   77-16711
ISBN 0-684-15527-3

This book published simultaneously in the
United States of America and in Canada—
Copyright under the Berne Convention

All rights reserved. No part of this book
may be reproduced in any form without the
permission of Charles Scribner's Sons.

1 3 5 7 9 11 13 15 17 19 M/P 20 18 16 14 12 10 8 6 4 2

Printed in the United States of America

My thanks to Maggie Lane, who like myself inherited old patterns from her mother and graciously shared them with me; to Jean Simpson, who rendered my penciled X's into clear and workable graphs; and especially to Janet Hornberger, whose professional skill and personal concern have guided me from start to finish.

Most of the letters and numbers in this book have been copied from old pattern books, an inheritance from the last century. People must have had better eyesight then, as the patterns are on a very small scale, some as small as thirty-five stitches (squares) to the inch. Many of them omitted the letter **J**, as **I** and **J** were usually considered interchangeable, as were **U** and **V** occasionally. I have supplied the missing **J** in most cases. By reproducing the patterns here on the scale of ten stitches to the inch and by not blacking in the squares completely it is hoped that they will be much more legible for today's embroiderers.

Originally the patterns were intended for cross-stitch markings on household linen or for little girls' samplers. Probably most people today will use them to personalize or sign pieces of needlepoint and for needlepoint "mottoes." Even if one is working the main part of the piece in tent stitch, it is sometimes advisable in the case of slender one-line letters to use cross-

stitch; be sure to slant the top cross in the same direction as the tent stitch, generally from lower left to upper right. Tent stitches will make a continuous line in one direction but a broken line in the other, and using cross-stitches will ensure a solid line. Cross-stitch, however, does require penelope or interlocked canvas.

The patterns start with letters five squares high, the minimum height, and range up to forty squares high. As shown on a ten-square grid, these will measure from ½ inch to 4 inches. Obviously, by using a coarser or finer canvas they can be made larger or smaller. While height remains uniform (except for ascenders and descenders on lowercase latters), width varies, the narrowest letter being **I**, the widest letters **M** and **W**.

When planning even the simplest monogram, block it out on graph paper to get the letters in the right relation to each other. You will find that some letters are more manageable than others: the symmetrical letters **A, H, I, M, O, S, T, U, V, W, X, Y,** and **Z** are easy; **B, C, D, E, G, K, L, N, Q,** and **R** at least sit firmly on their bases; **F** and **P** are top-heavy; and **J** always looks as if it would tumble to the right. **J** works best as the first letter of a monogram, **L** as the last; **F** and **P** are difficult in any position.

Monograms most often consist of three letters but frequently of only two. A four-letter monogram is exceptional and does not allow much variation in the grouping of the letters. To play down the middle letters is one solution, for example J$_{\check{C}}^{V}$P . For two letters, try interlacing them, using alphabets 25 and 27; or rounded, with or without a framing circle, as in alphabet 21 €D ; or boxed M/W .

For a three-letter monogram, the third (surname) initial is often put in the middle, with the first and second on either side and smaller A**S**L , or both on one side $_B^A$**N** ; slant downward in block or interlocking letters R**M**D ;

combine alphabets 21 and 22 €ID ; or think up your own combination.

In any case plan carefully and work out your design on paper. Use a soft pencil, No. 1 or No. 2, which will erase easily —and you'll be doing some of that—and have a clean, new eraser handy. Faber's "Pink Pearl" is recommended.

LETTERS
AND NUMBERS

1 Five-square minimum block capitals

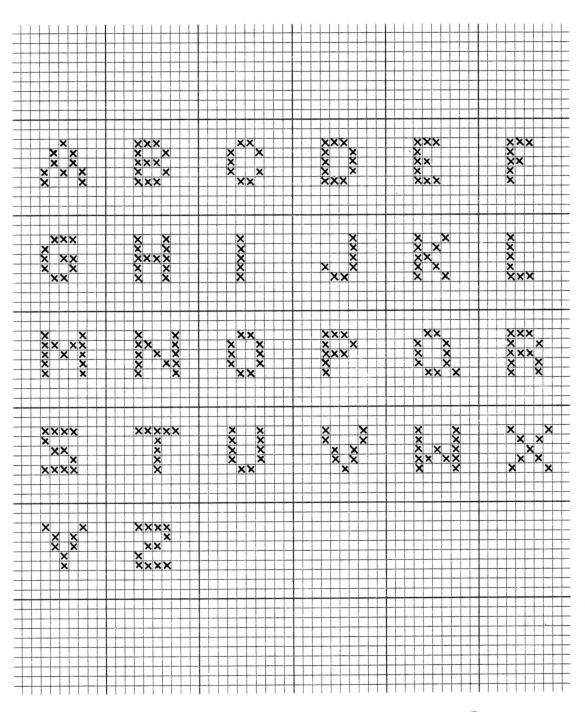

2 Five-square script with five-square ascenders, four-square descenders

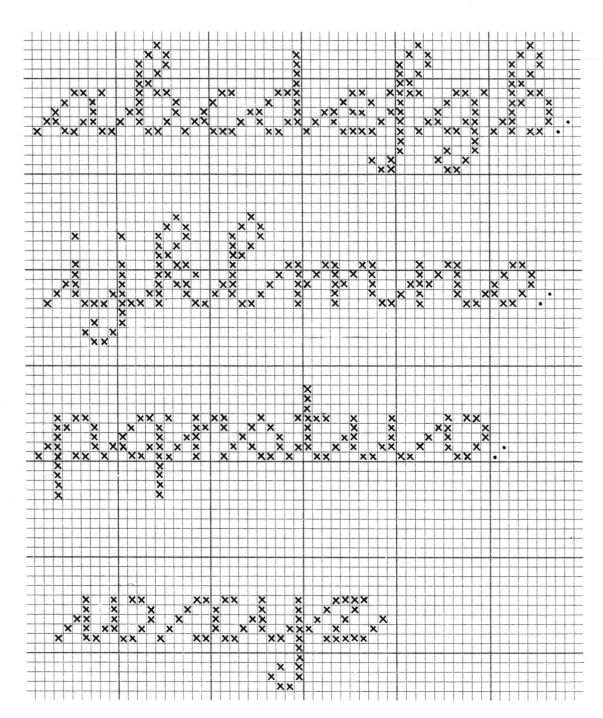

3 Five-square lowercase italic, with four-square ascenders and descenders

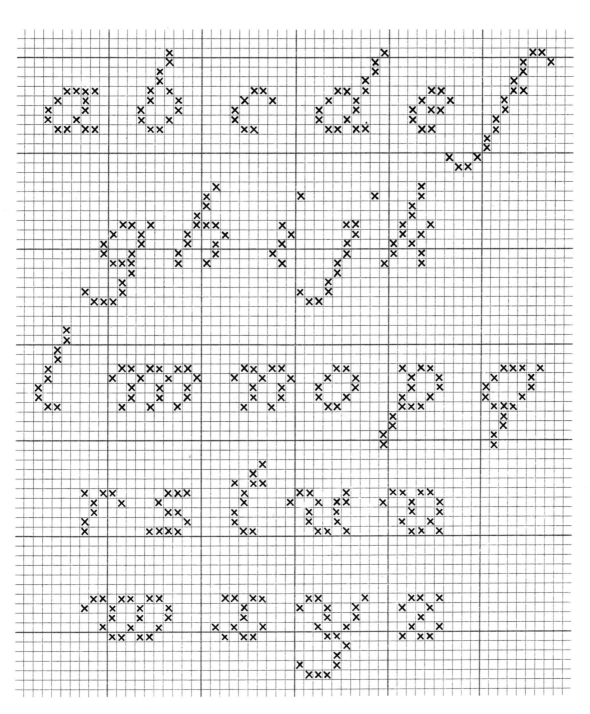

4 Six-square block capitals

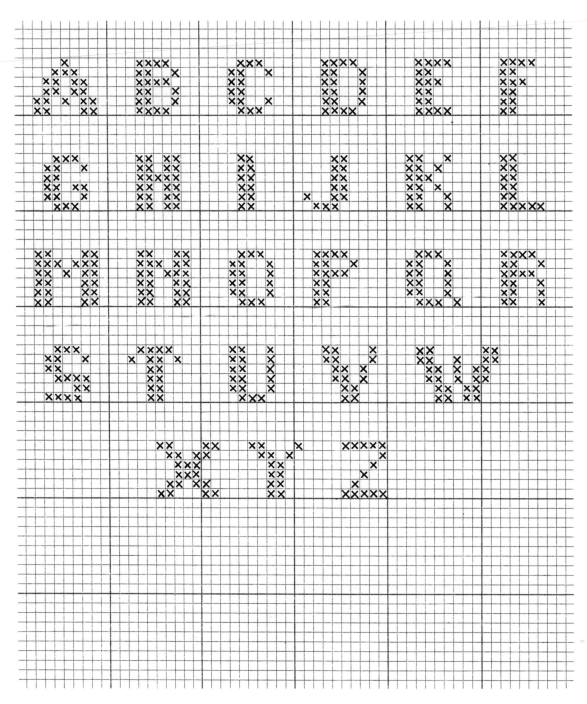

5 Seven-square open capitals

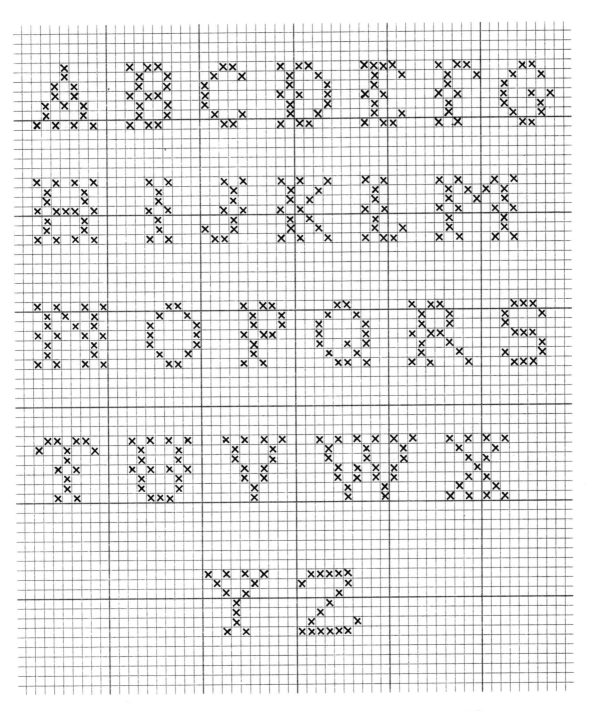

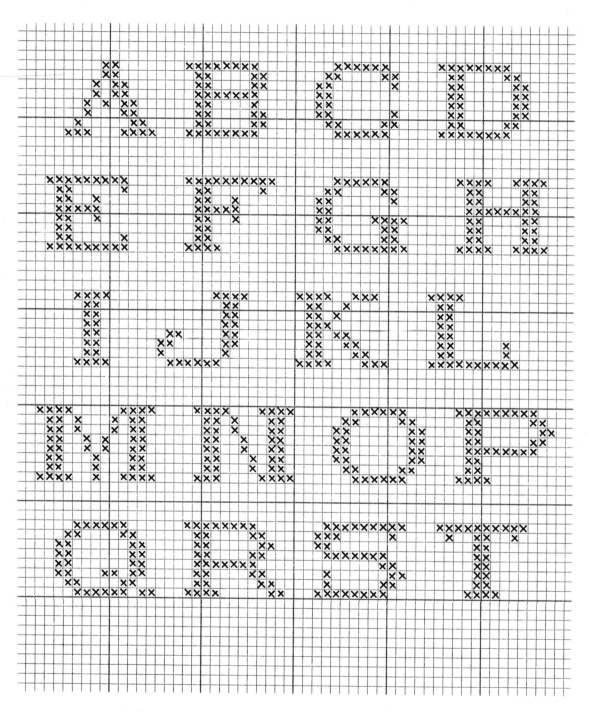

14

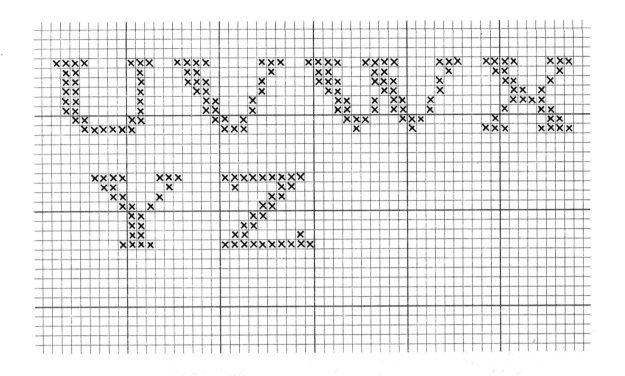

7 Nine-square block capitals

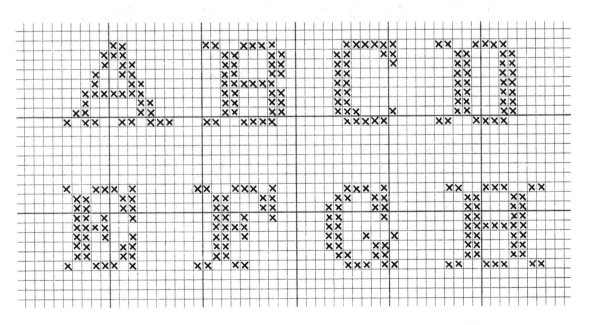

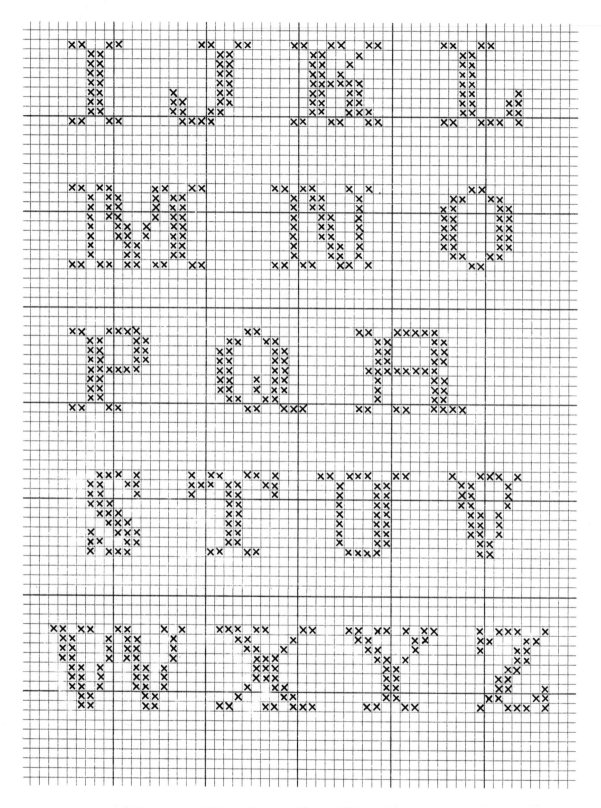

16

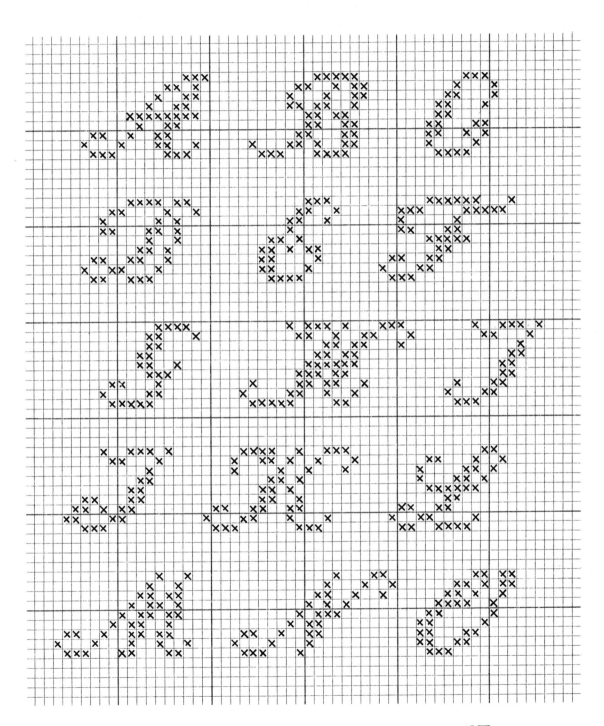

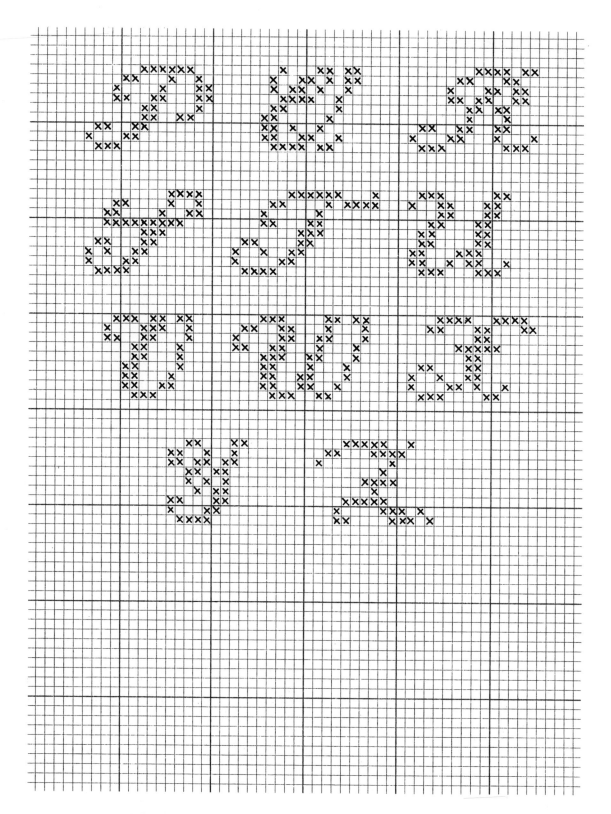

18

9 Nine-square lowercase gothic, with three ascenders and descenders

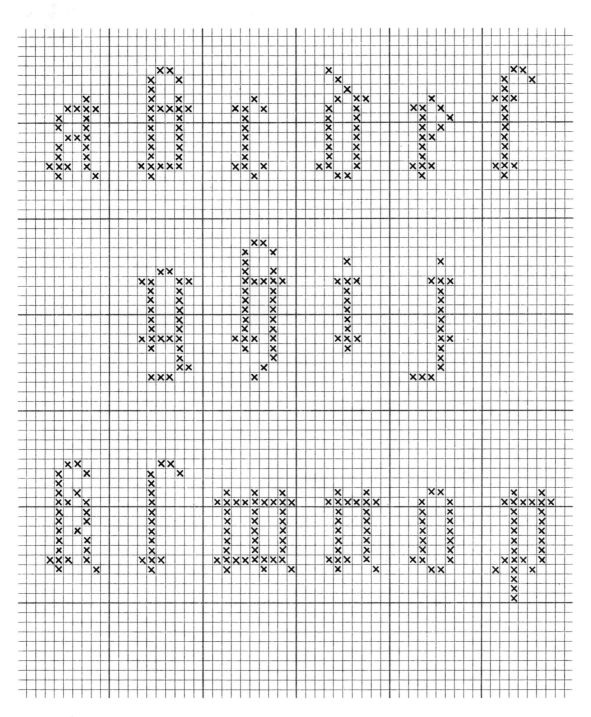

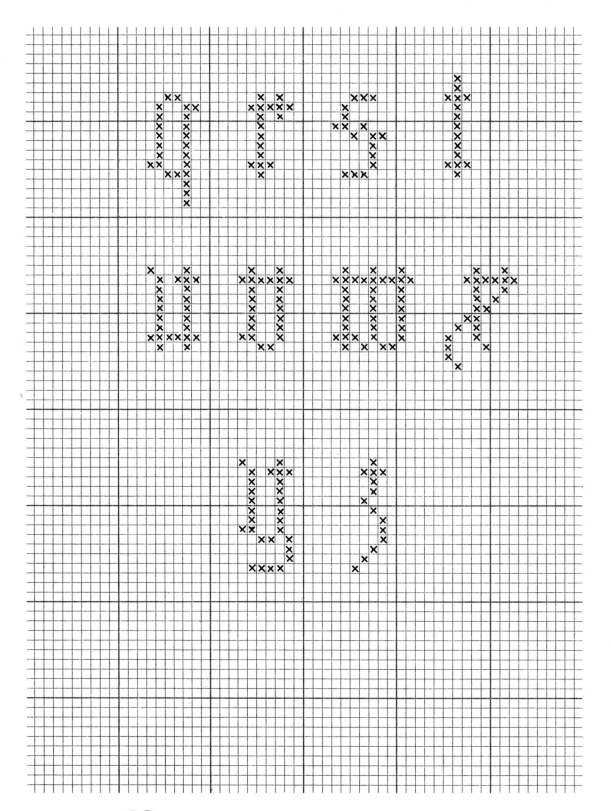

20

10 Nine-square lowercase gothic, with three ascenders and four descenders

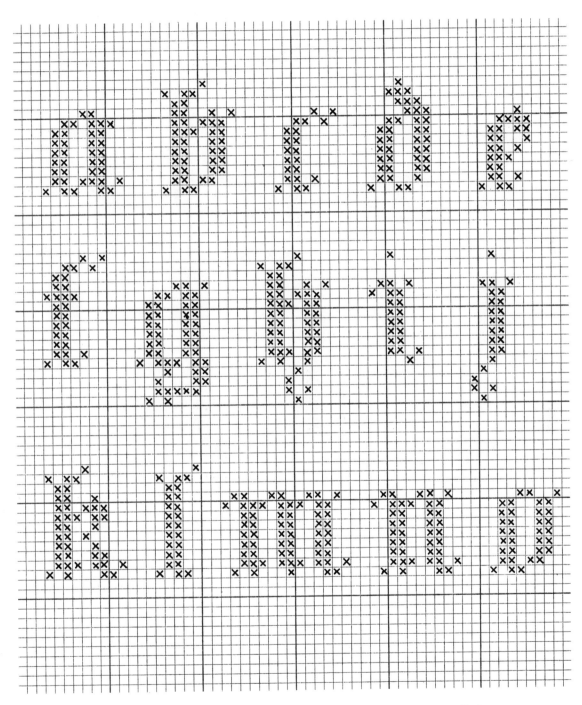

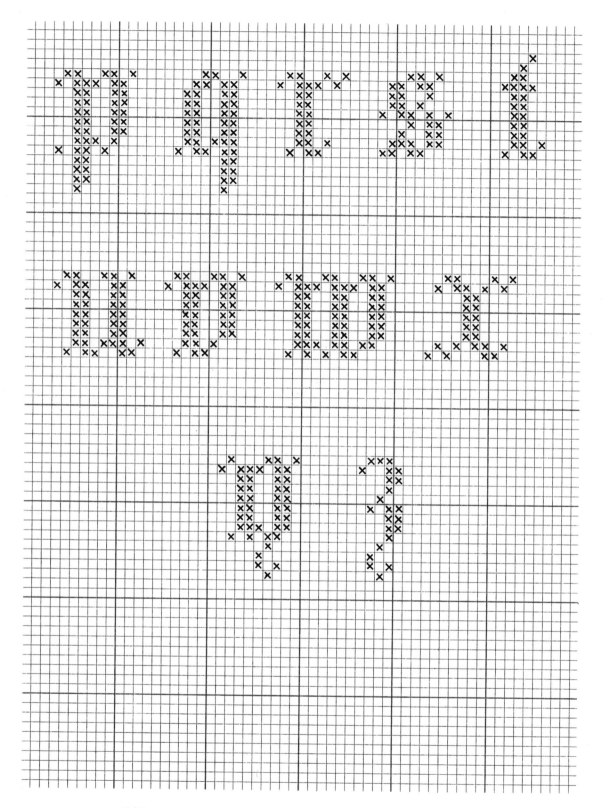

11 Ten-square block capitals

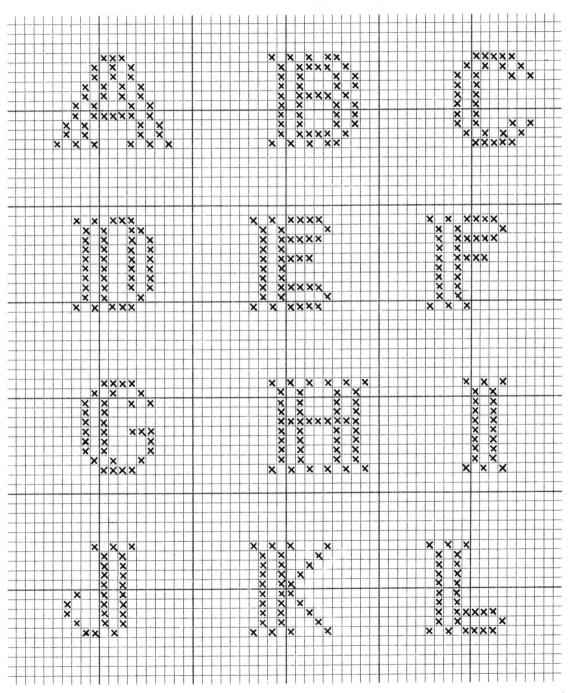

copied

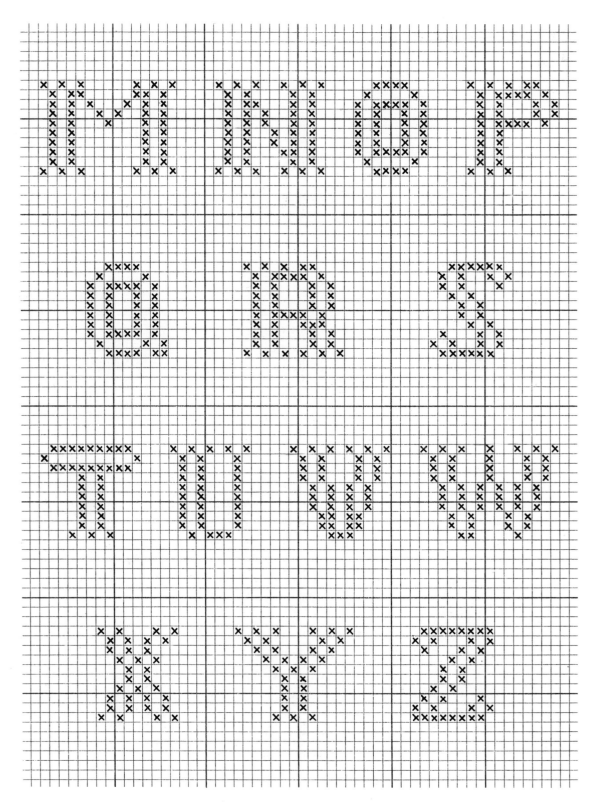

24 copied

Ten-square fancy capitals

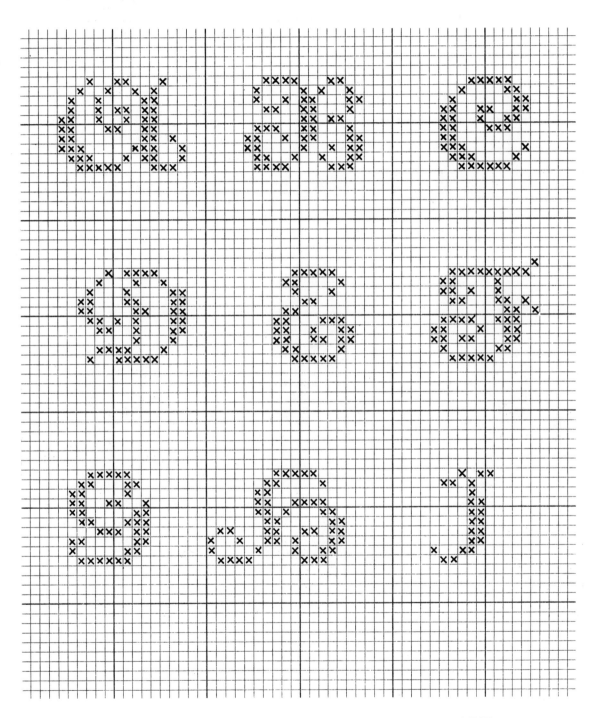

25

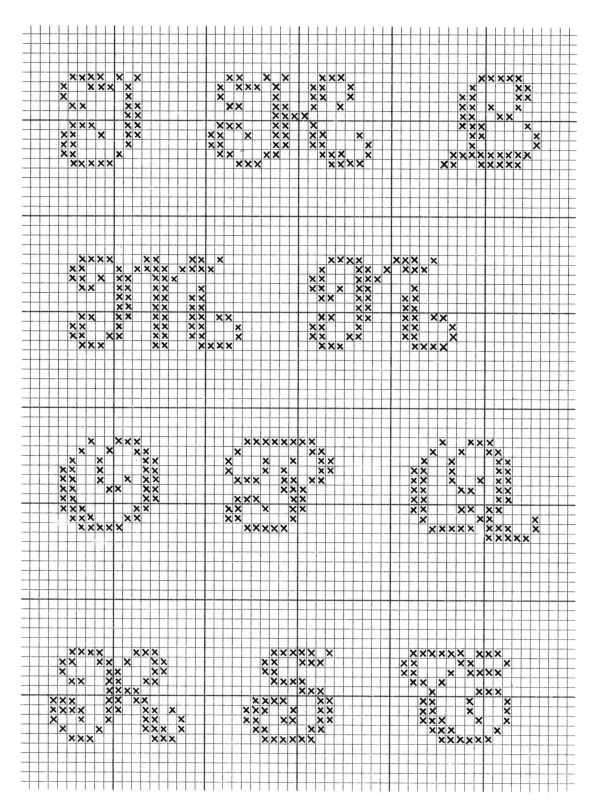

26

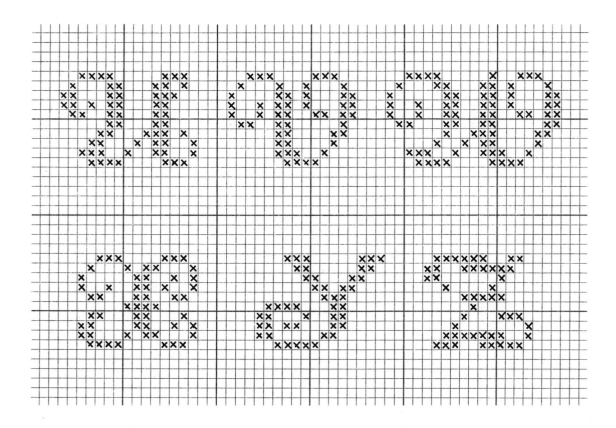

13 Ten-square lowercase italic, with eight ascenders and descenders

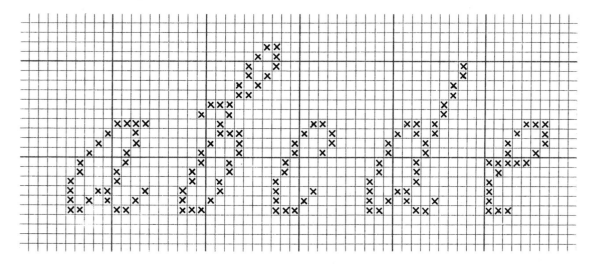

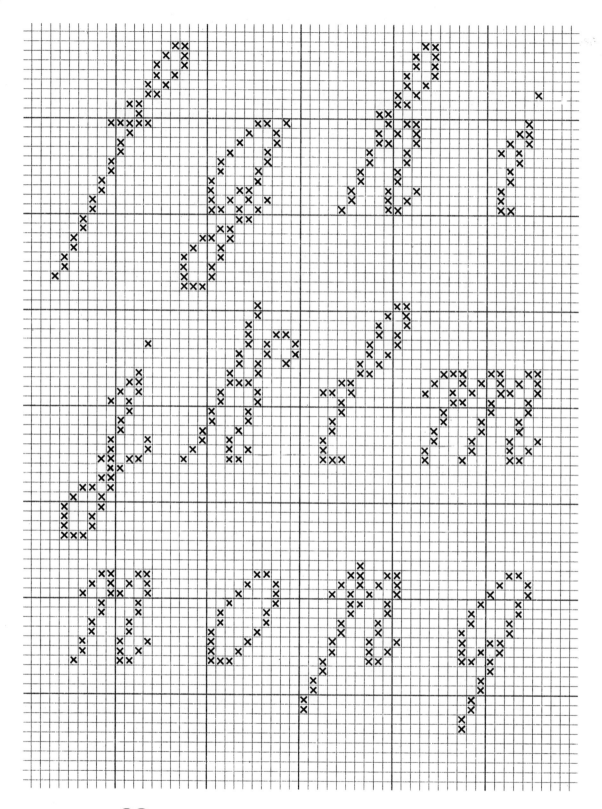

28

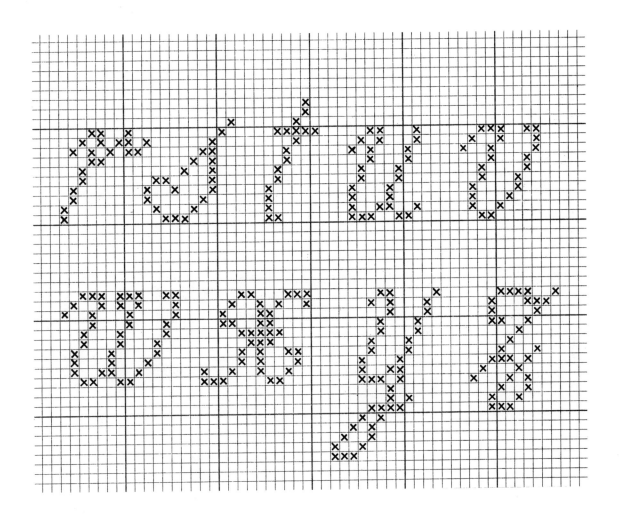

14 Eleven-square narrow block capitals

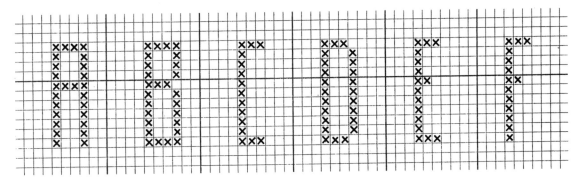

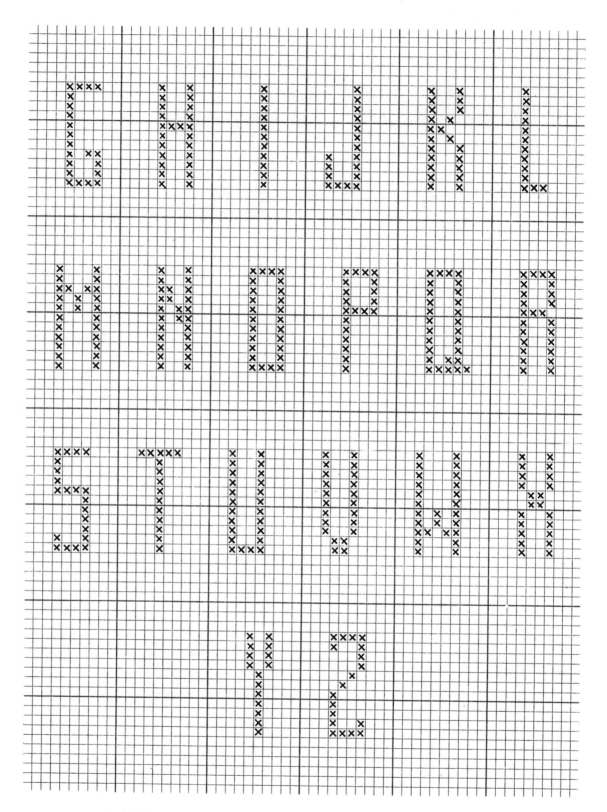

30

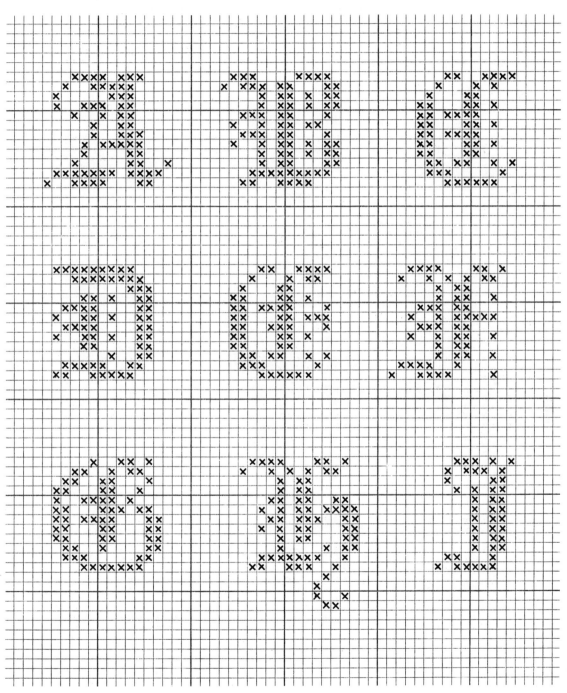

31 copied

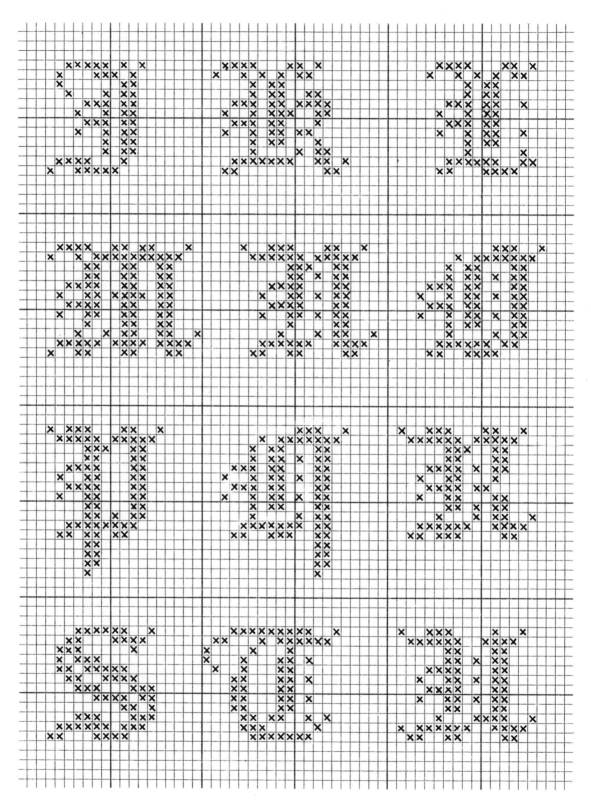

32 copied

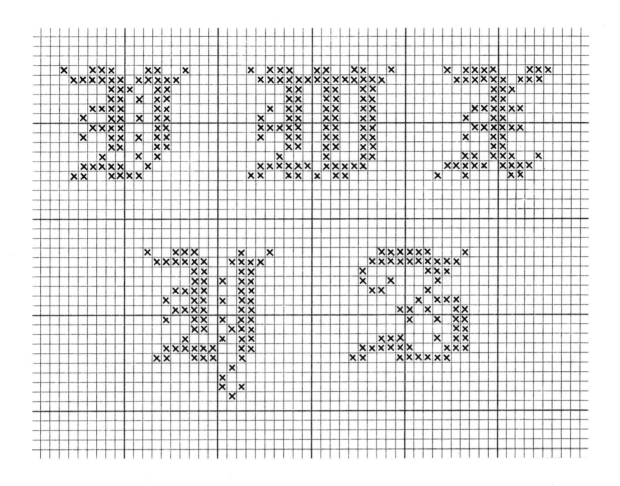

16 Twelve-square fancy capitals, two ascenders, four descenders

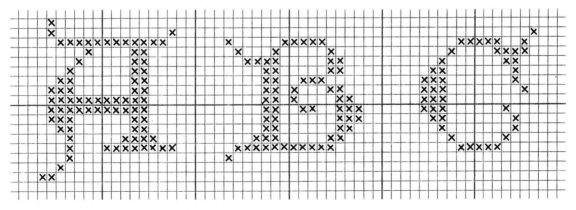

33 *copied.*

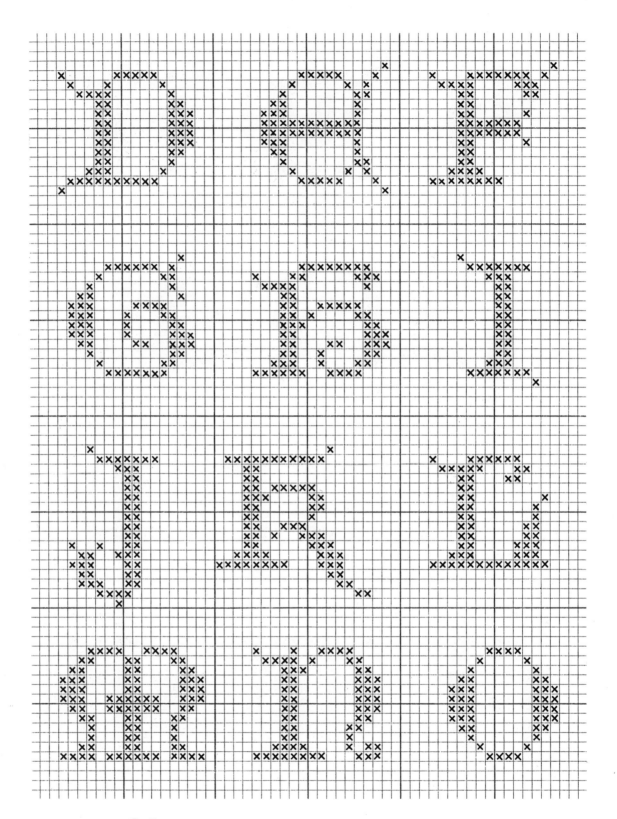

34

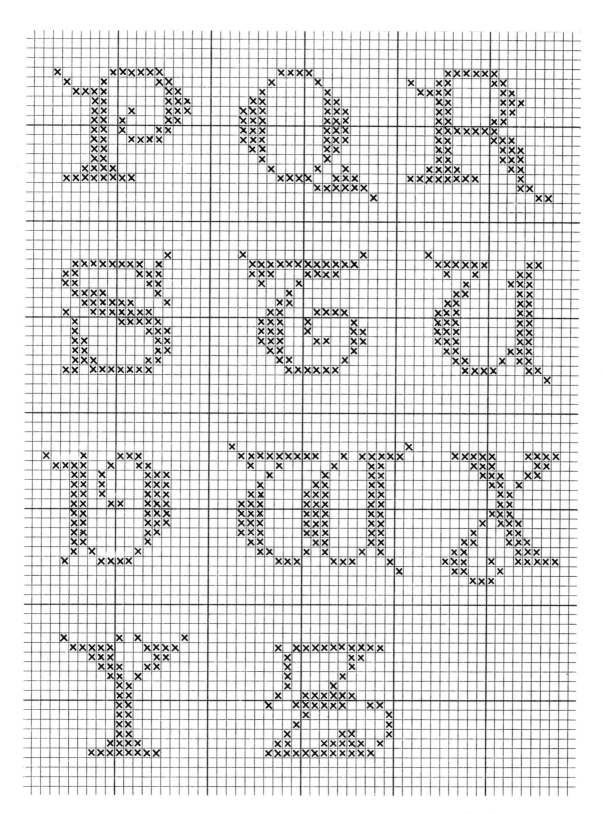

35

17 Twelve-square italic capitals, two ascenders, four descenders

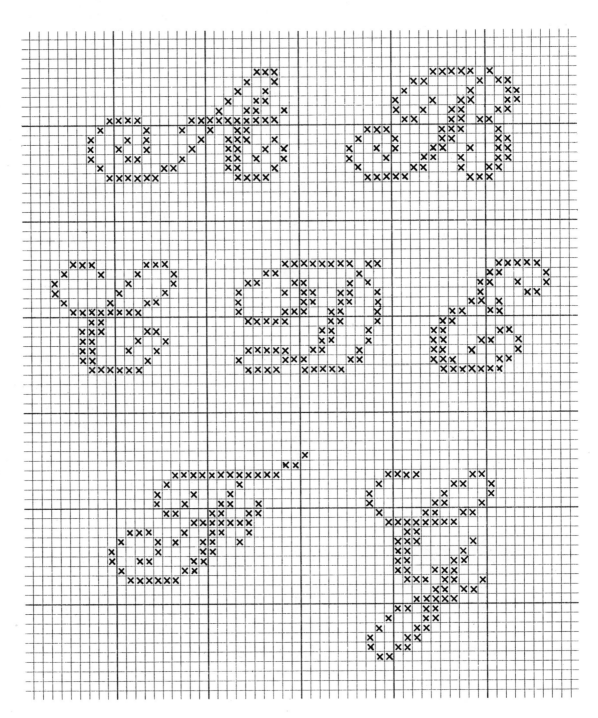

36

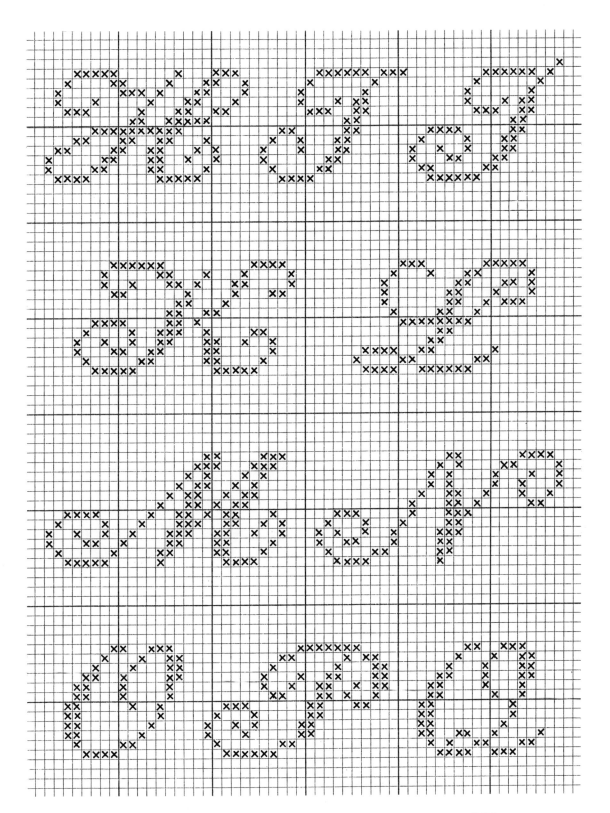

37

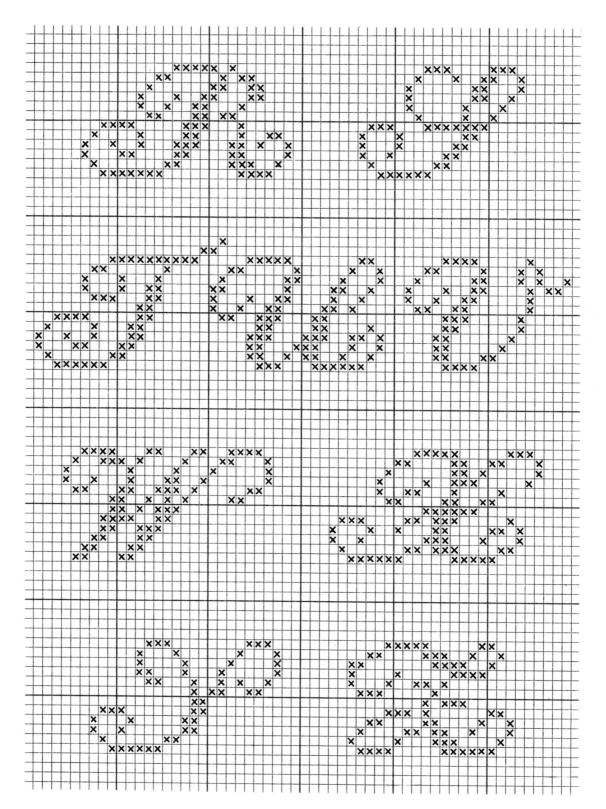

38

18 Twelve-square capitals on the bias

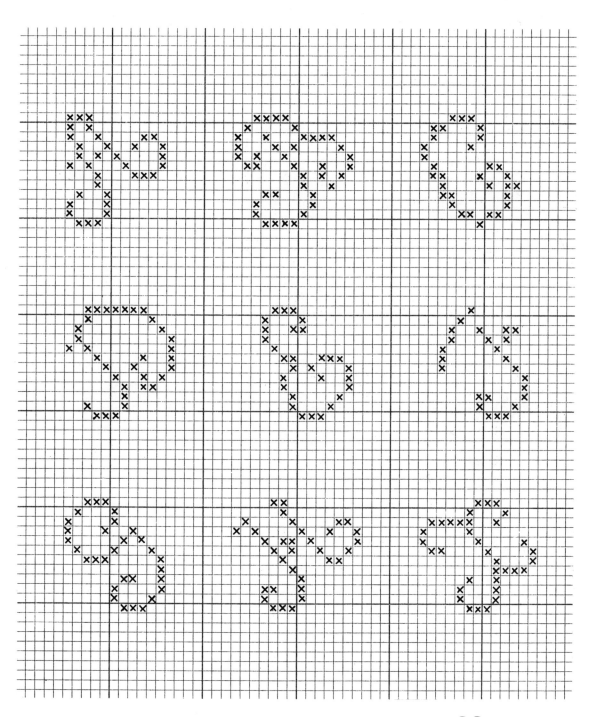

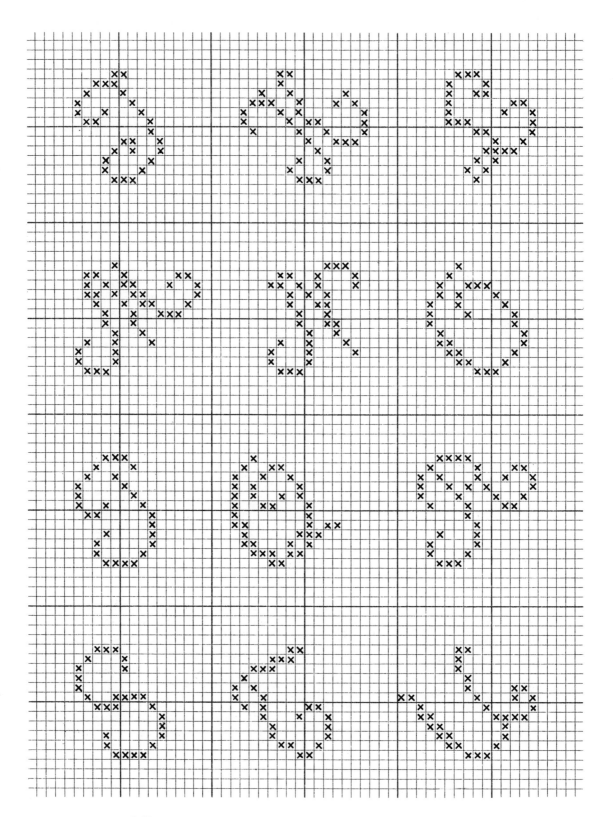

40

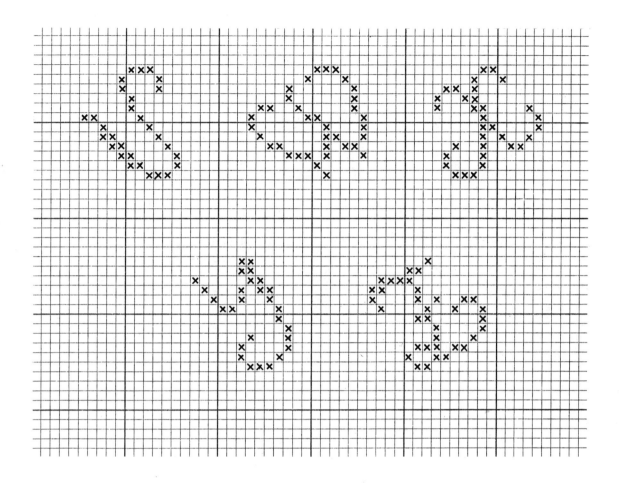

19 Thirteen-square block capitals with second color indication

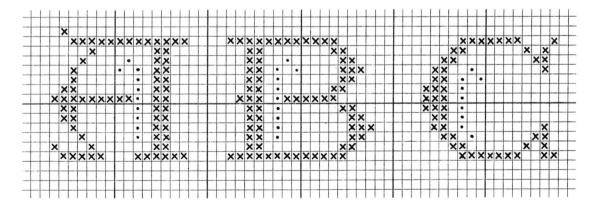

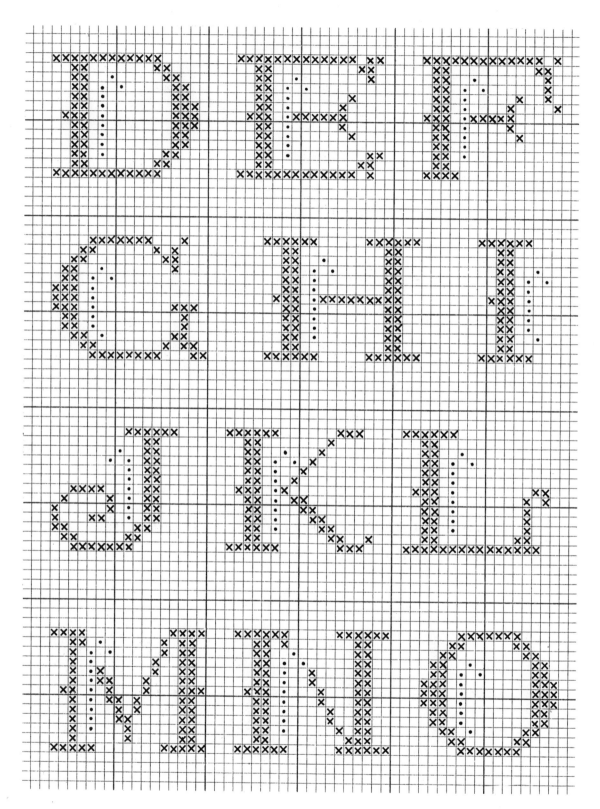

42

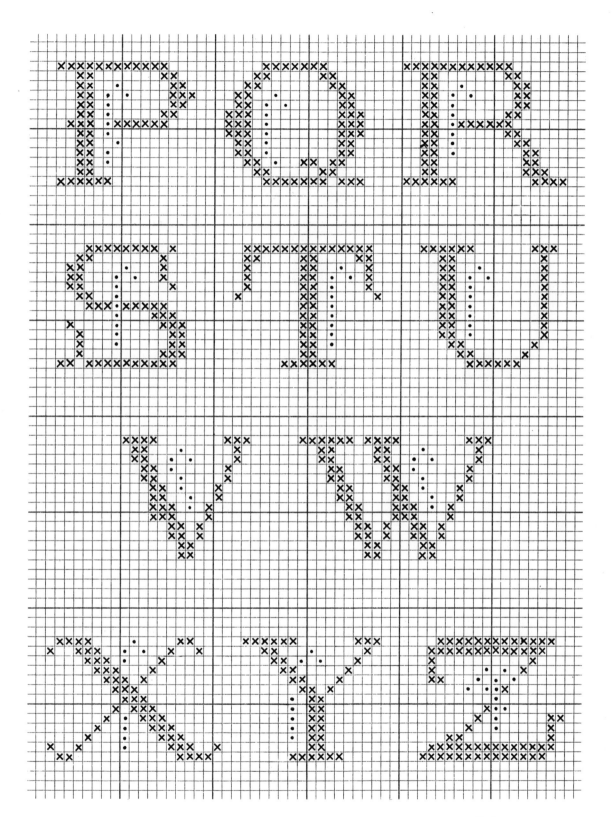

43

20 Thirteen-square heavy capitals

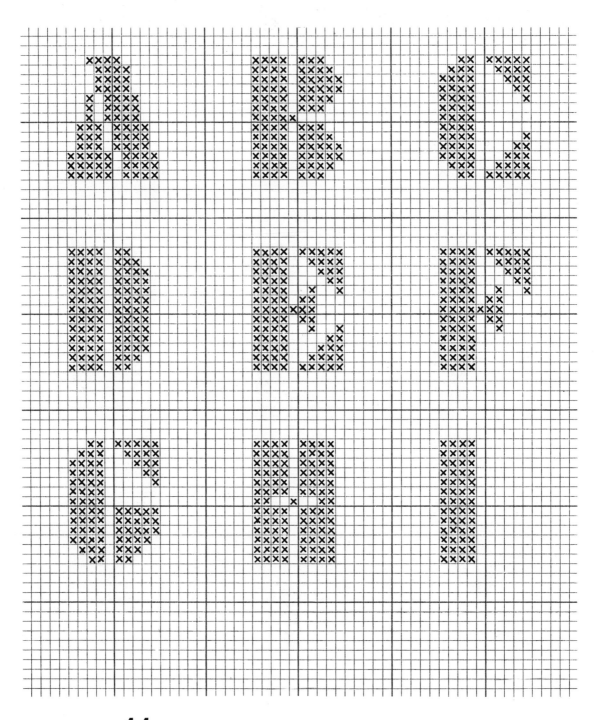

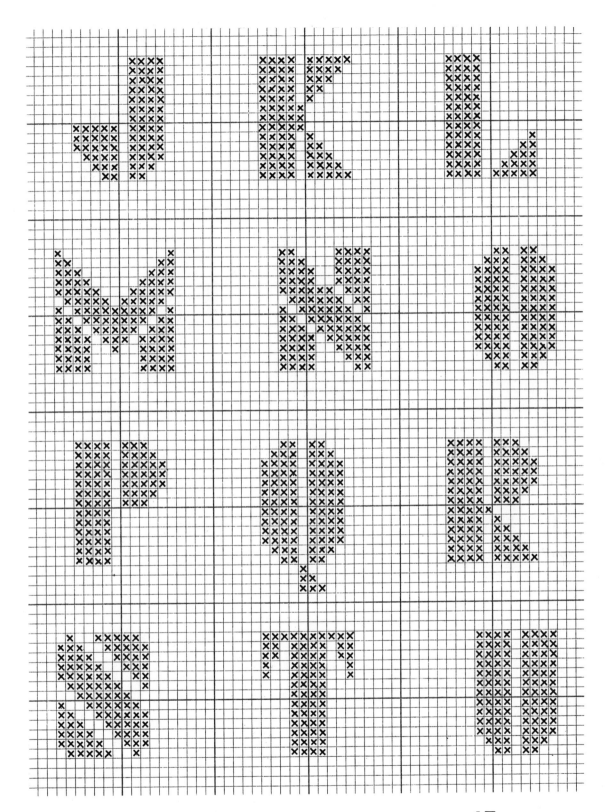

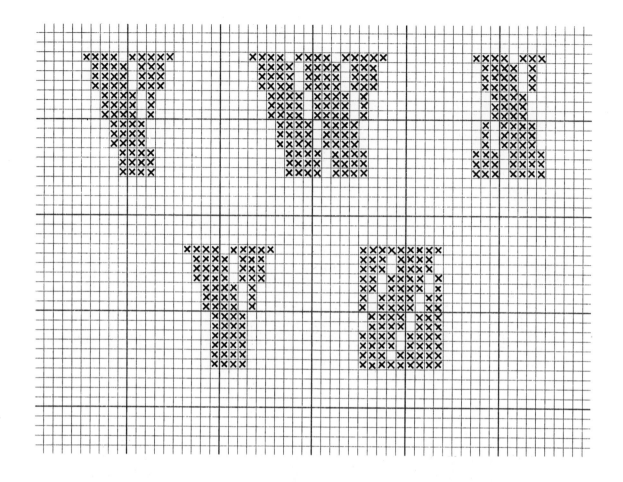

21 Thirteen-square capitals, half-rounded, facing both ways

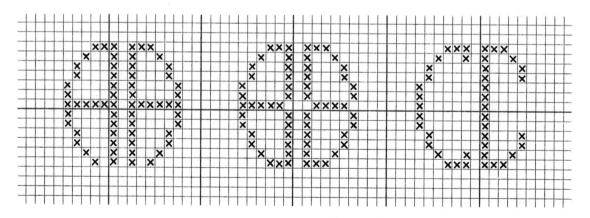

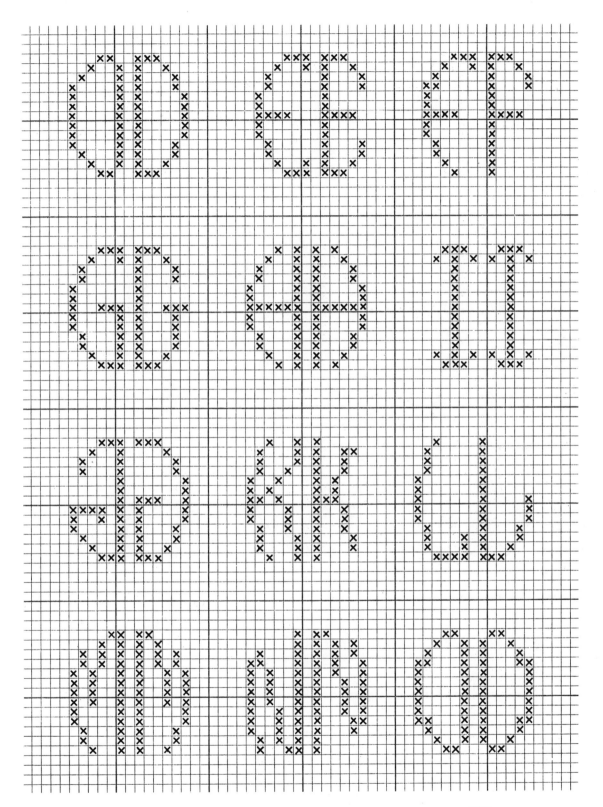

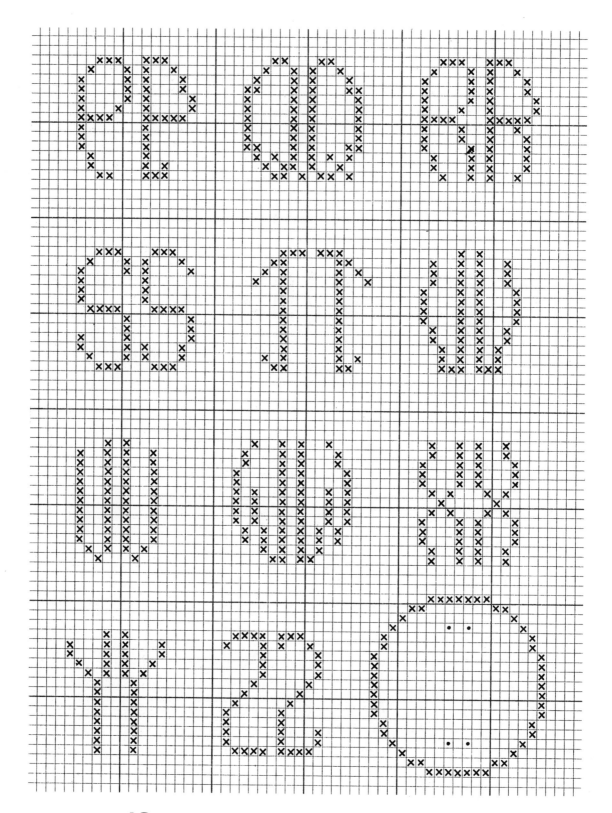

48

22 Thirteen-square plain capitals to match alphabet 21

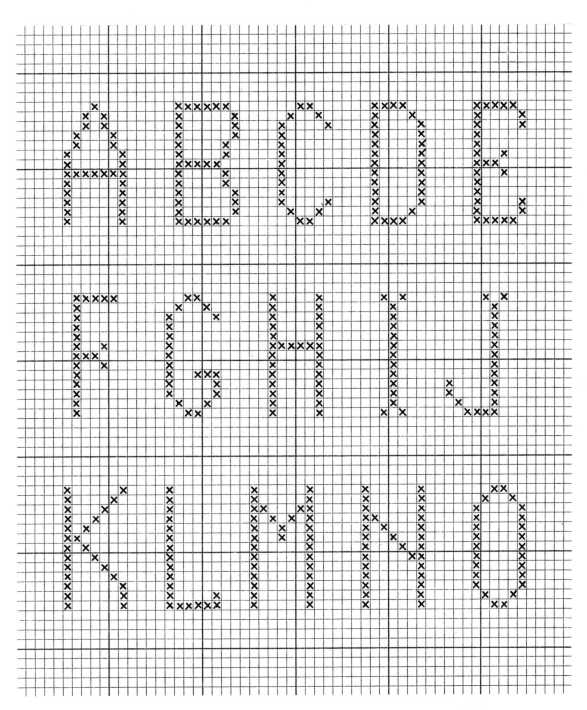

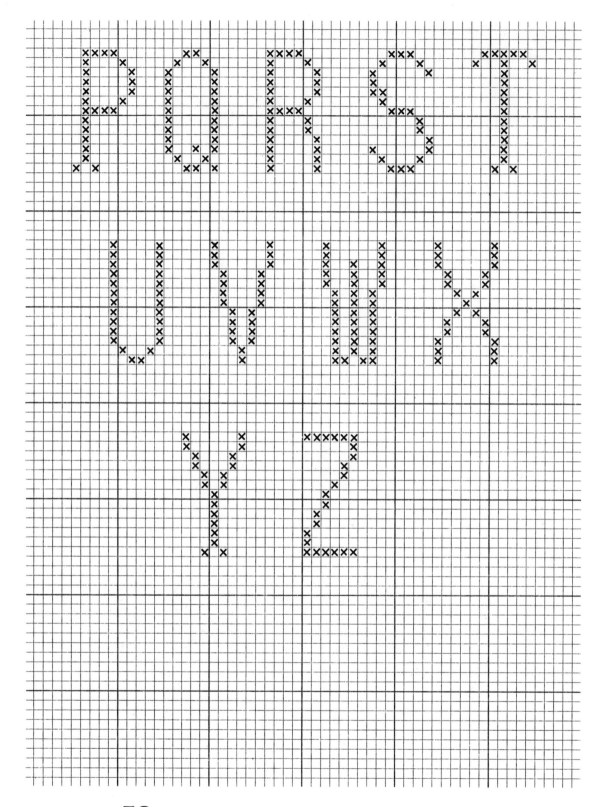

50

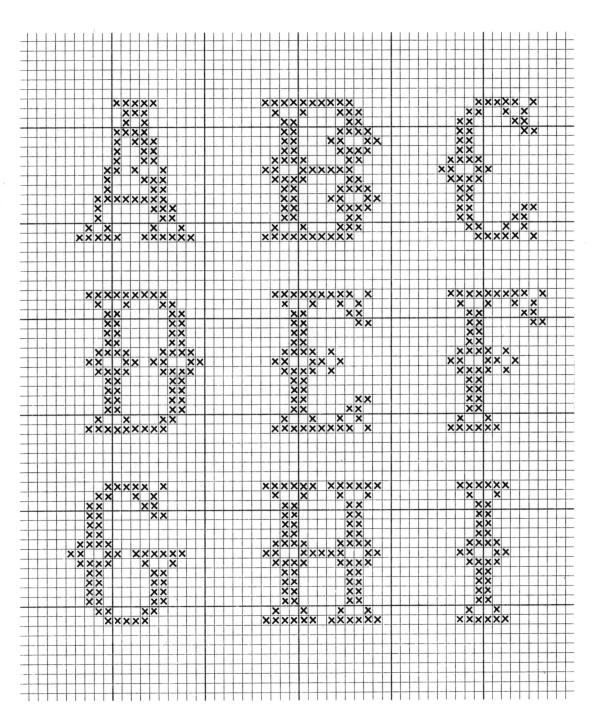

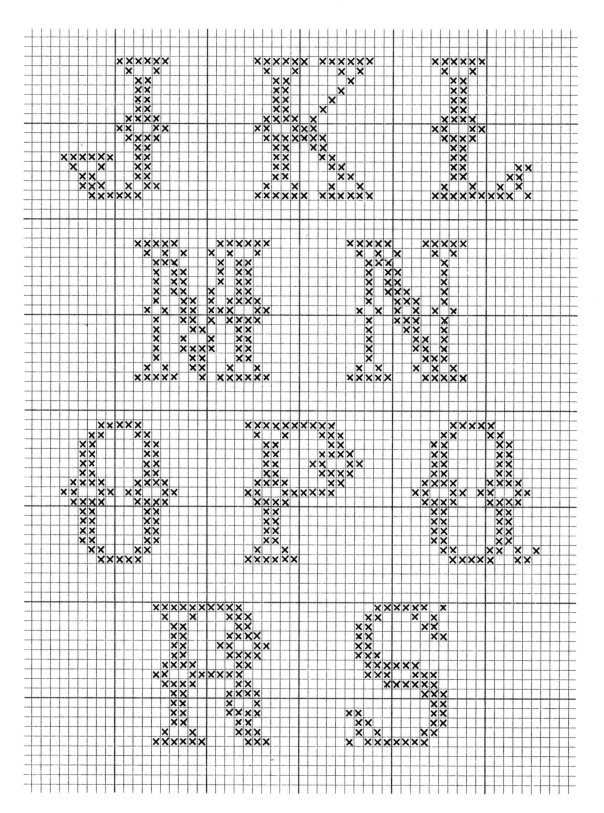

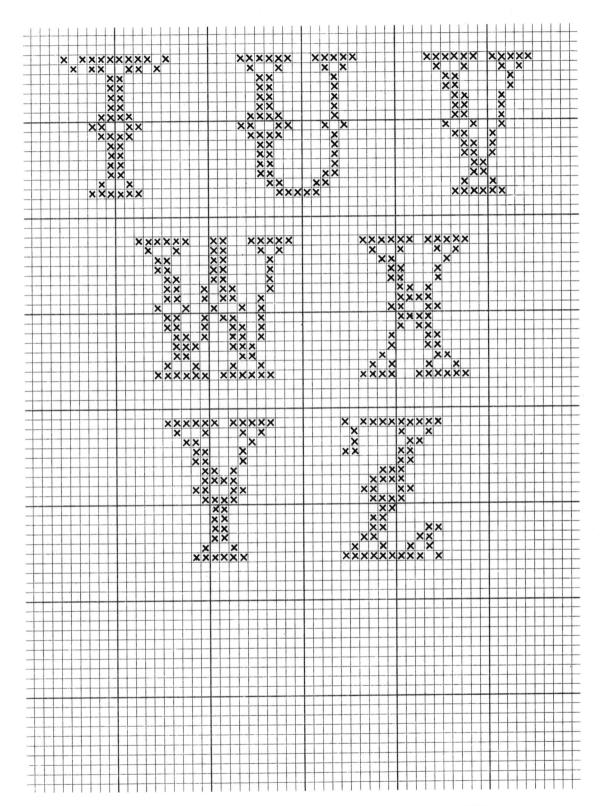

53

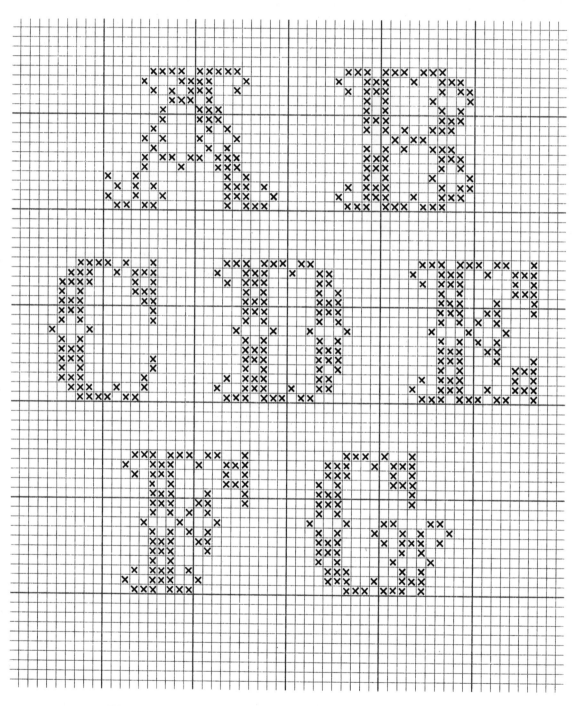

copied 54

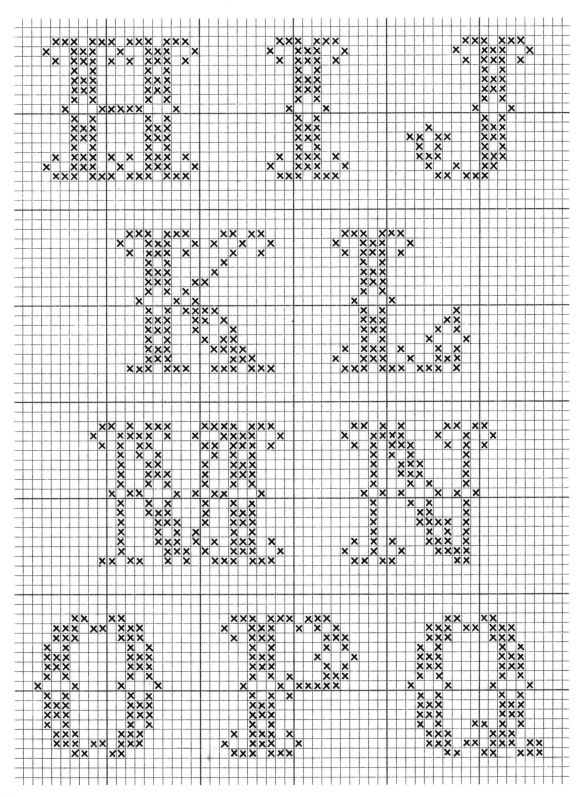

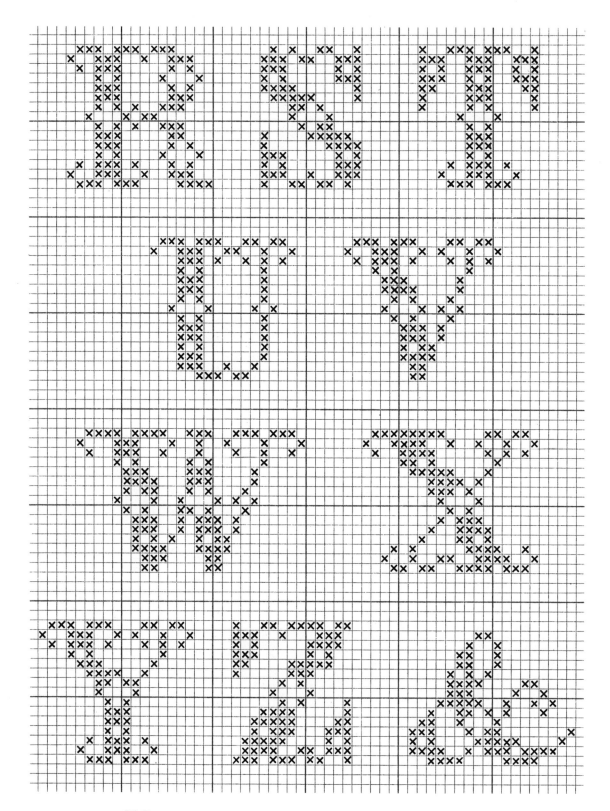

56

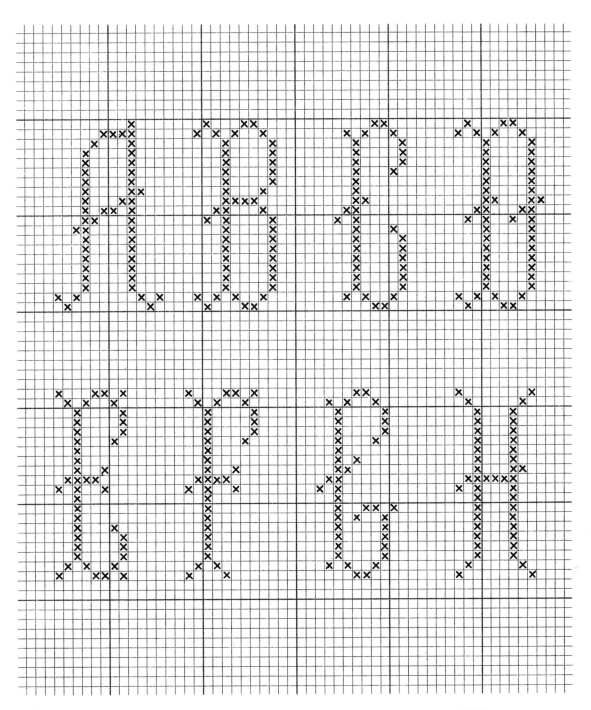

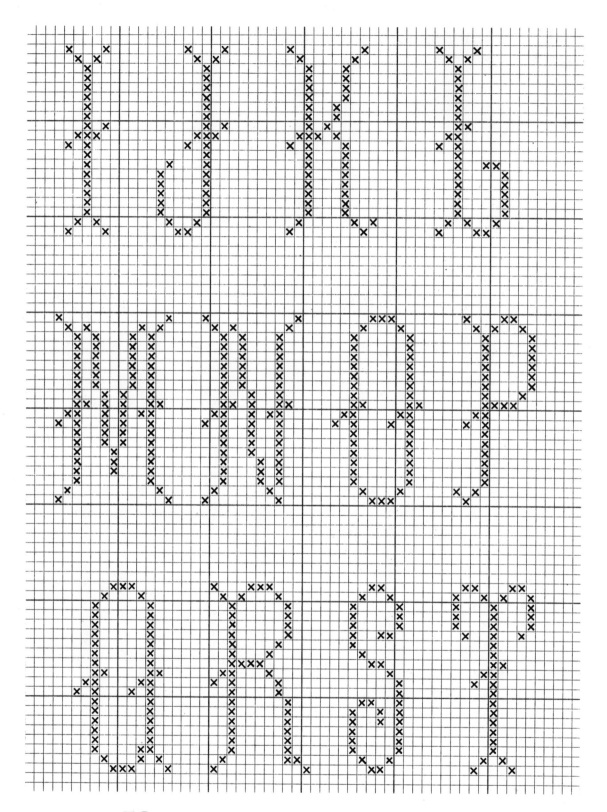

58

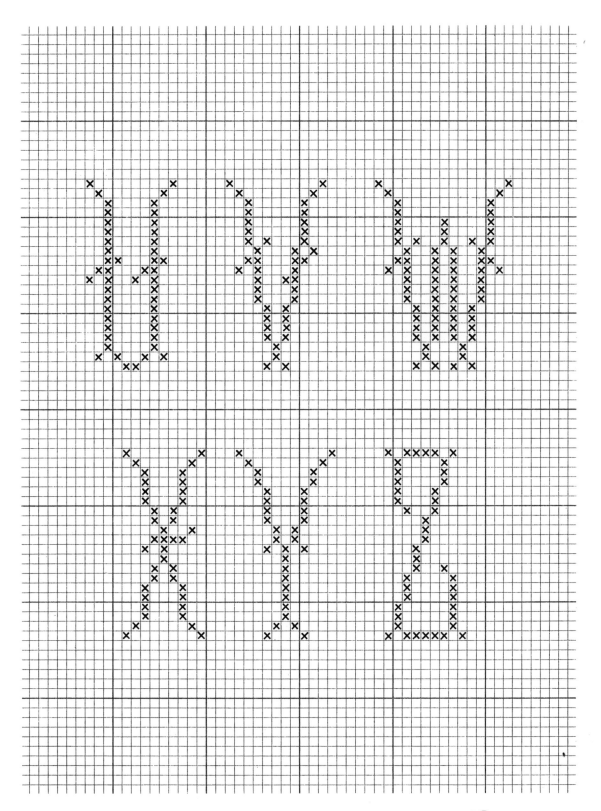

59

26 Twenty-square open block capitals
(can be interwoven with alphabet 27)

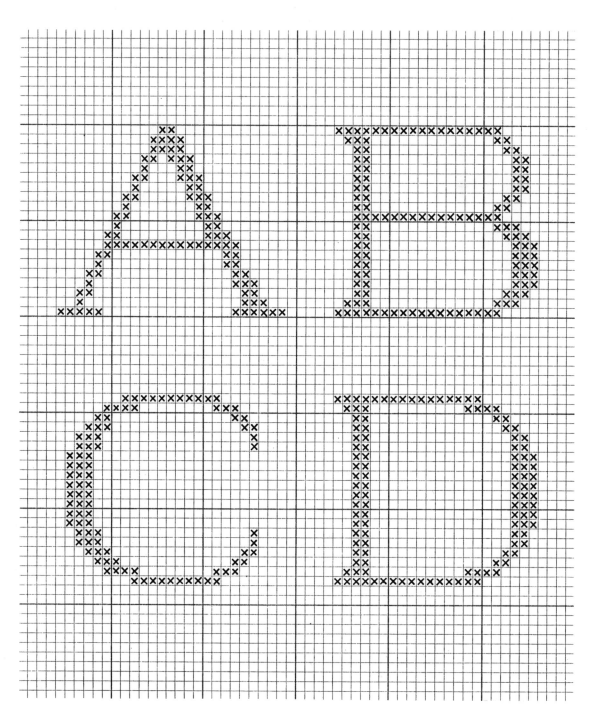

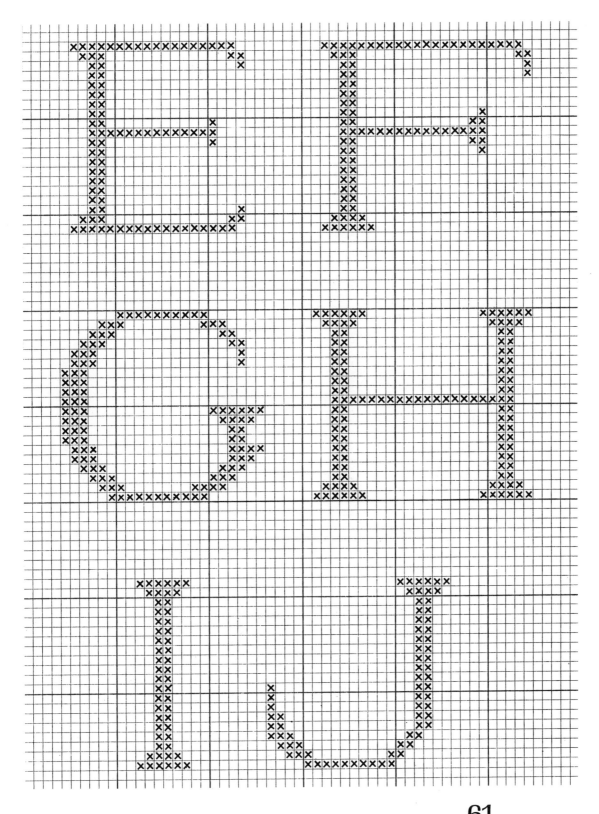

61

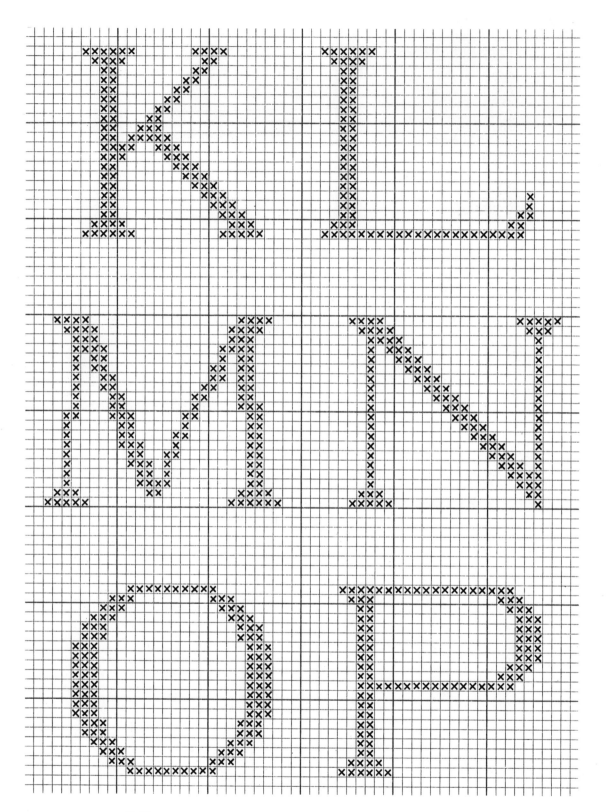

62

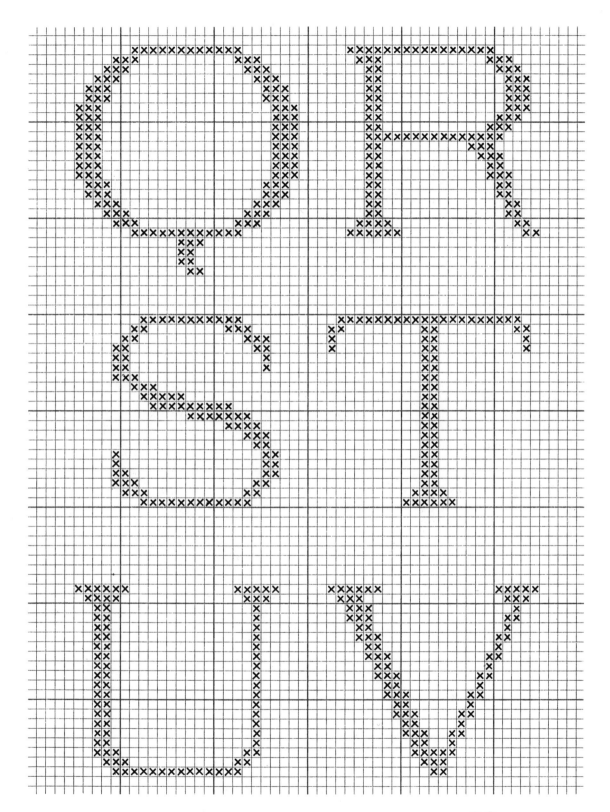

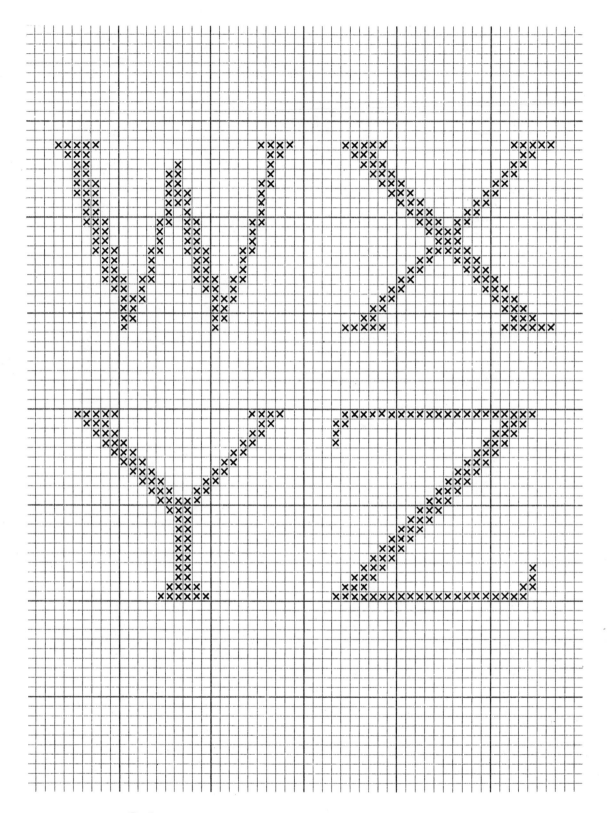

64

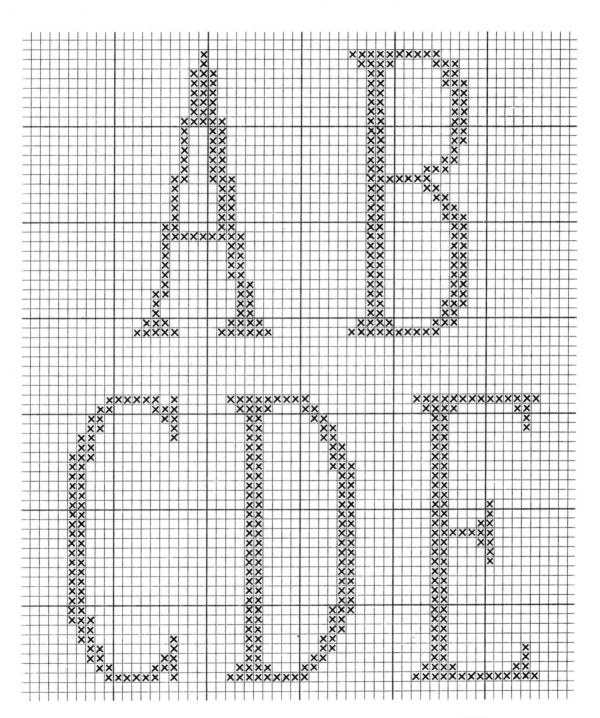

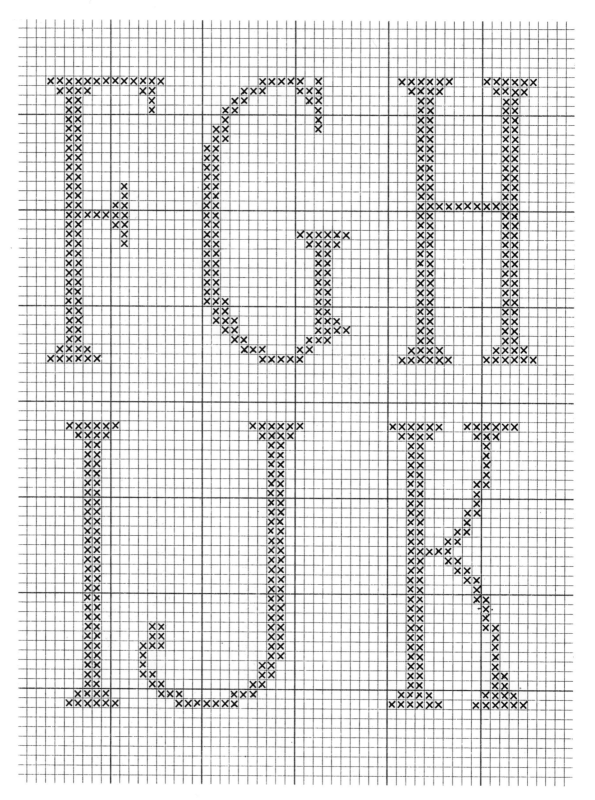

66

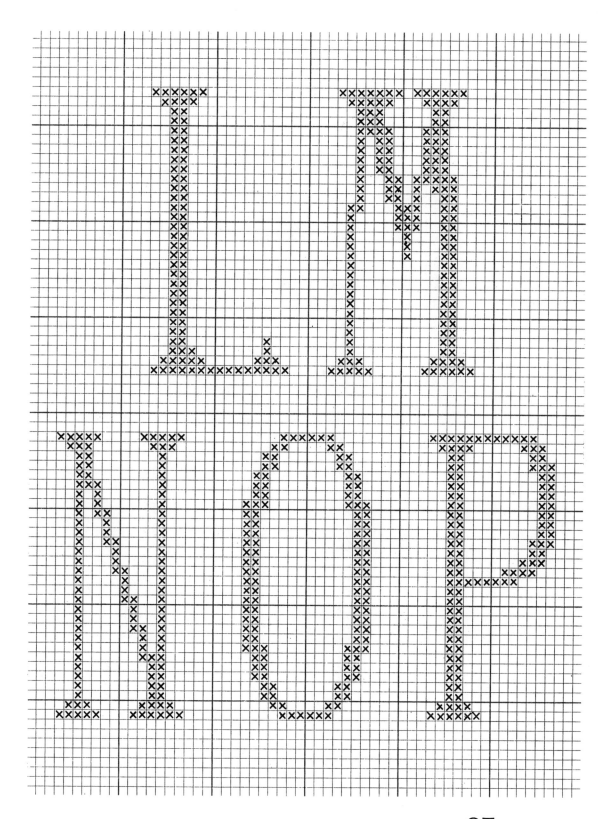

67

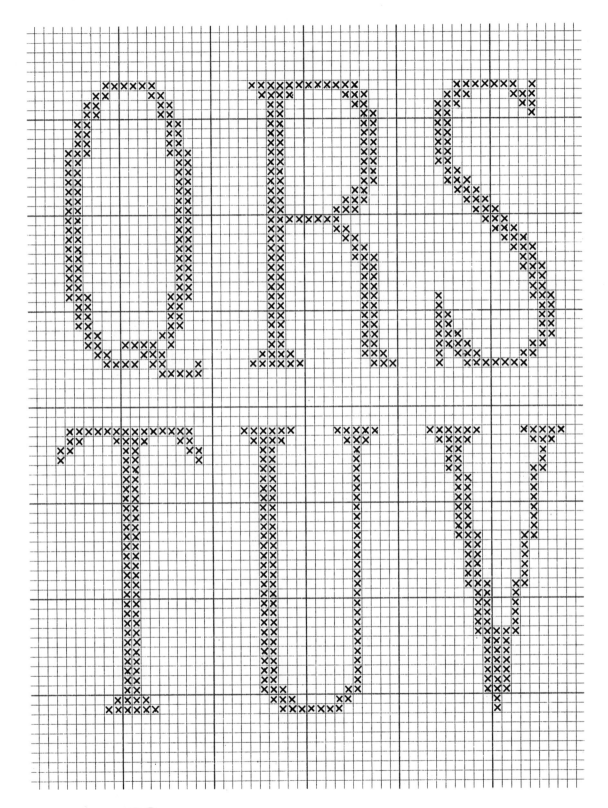

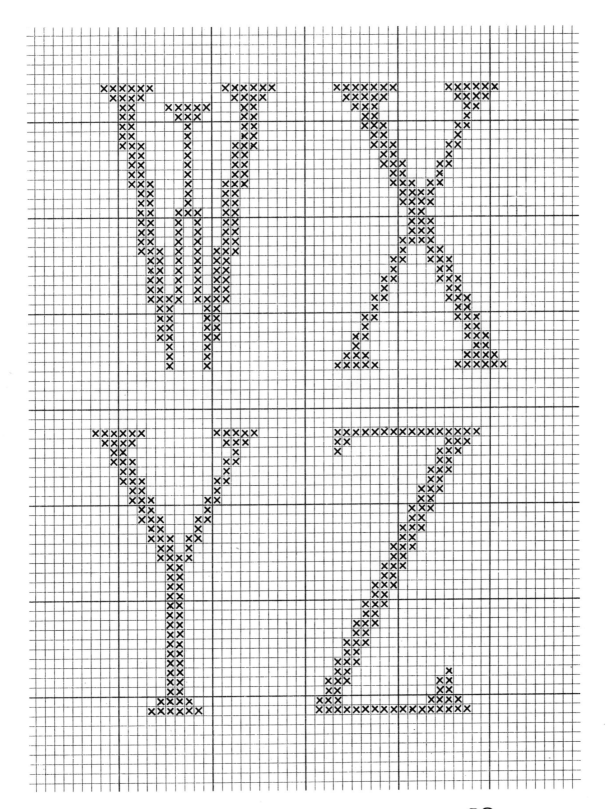

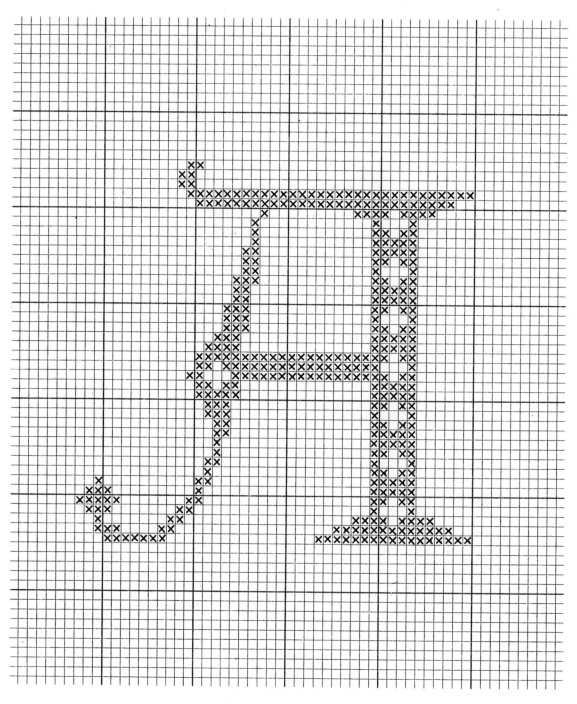

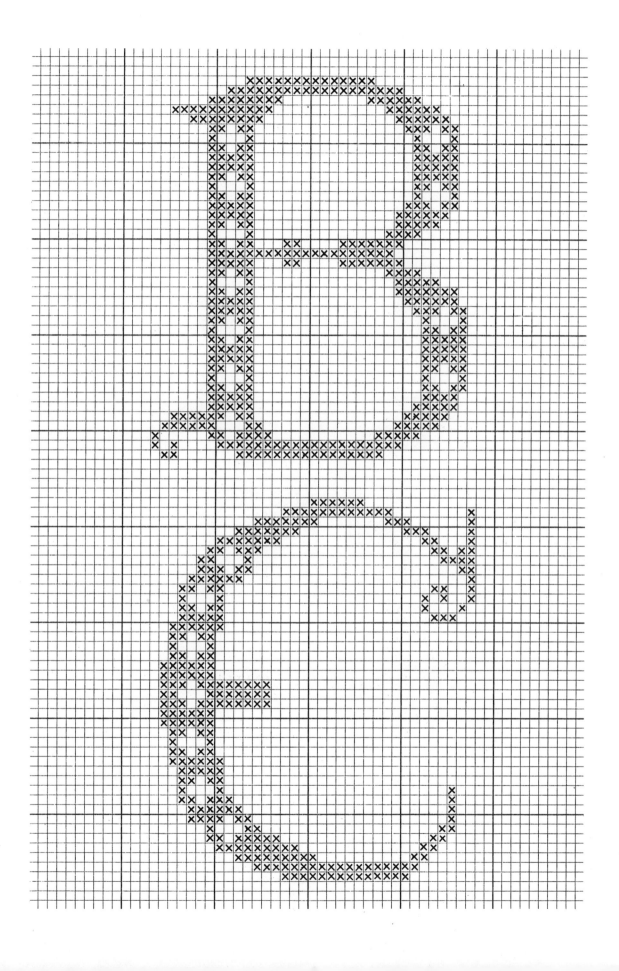

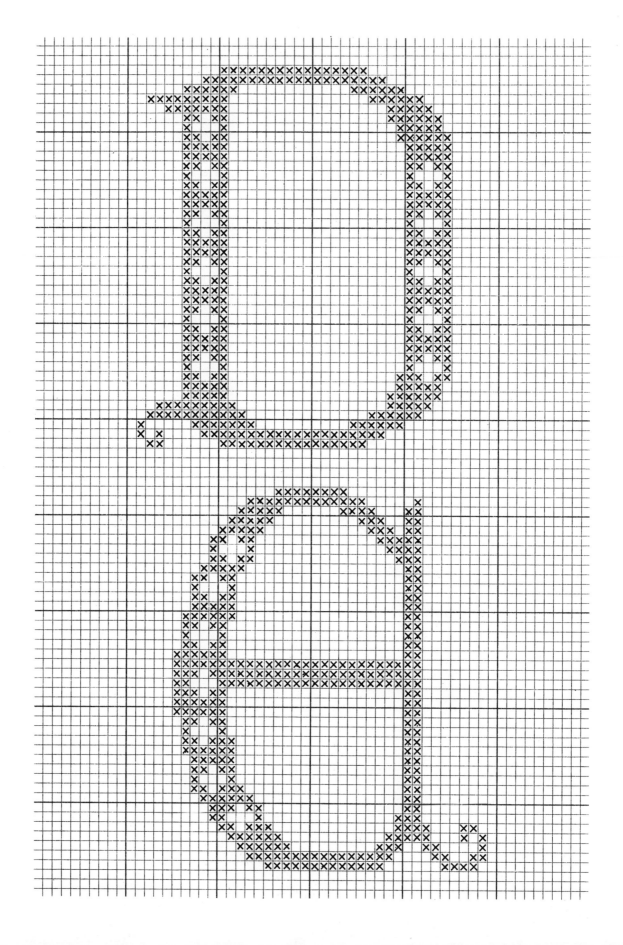

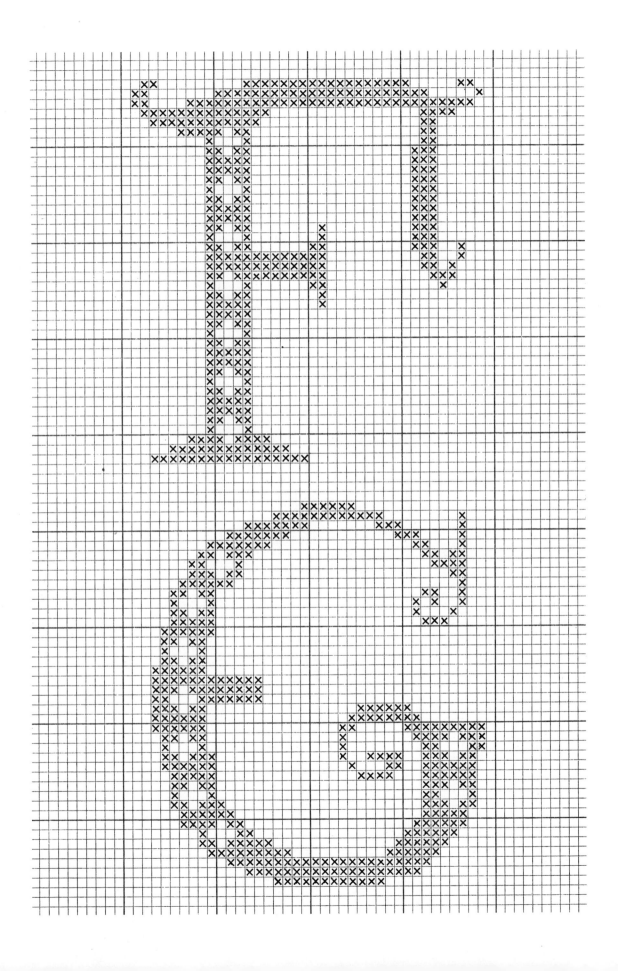

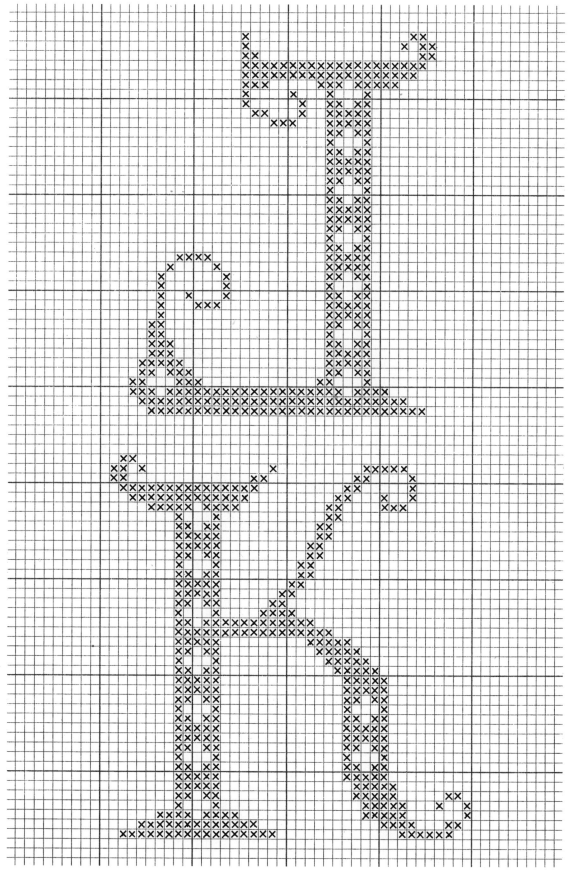

copied

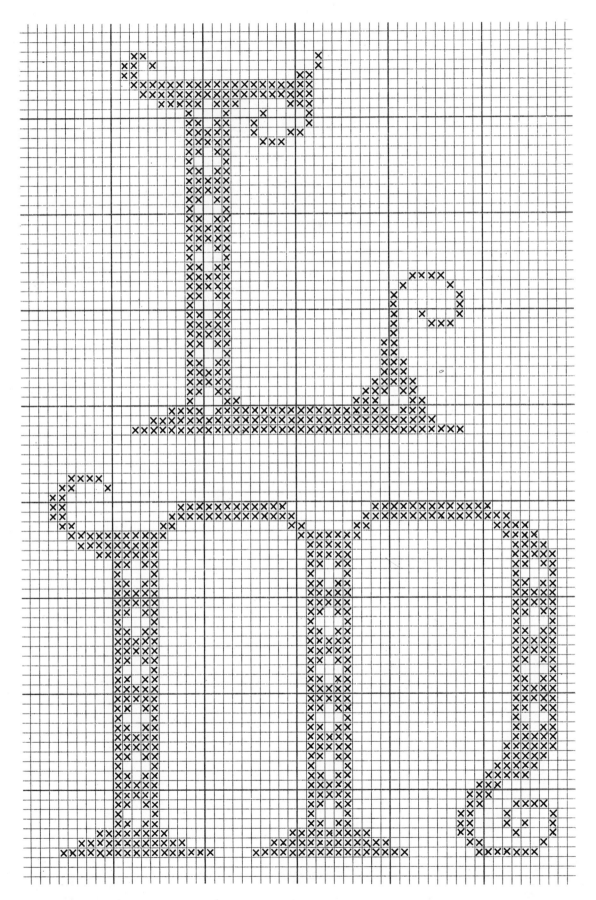

copied

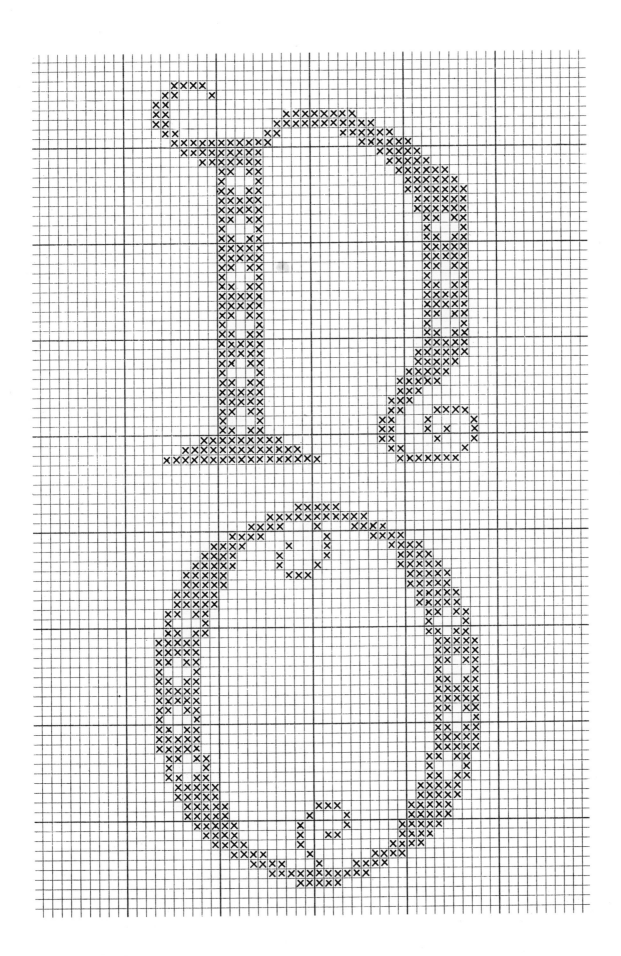

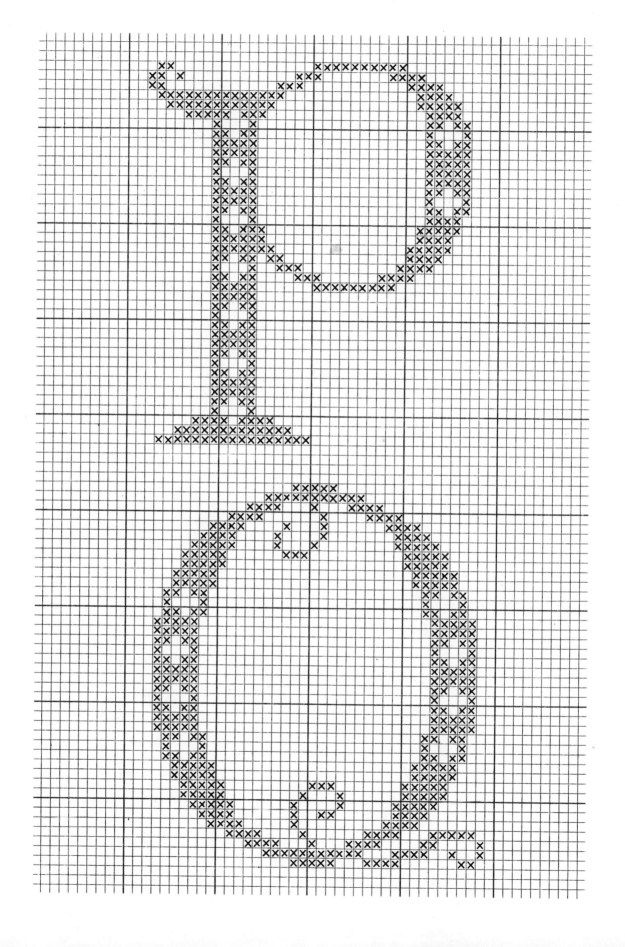

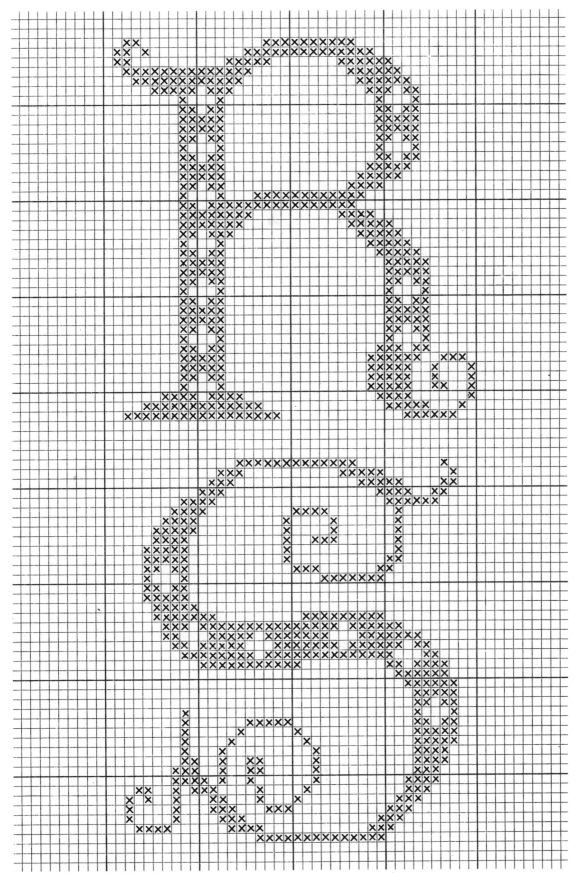

copier

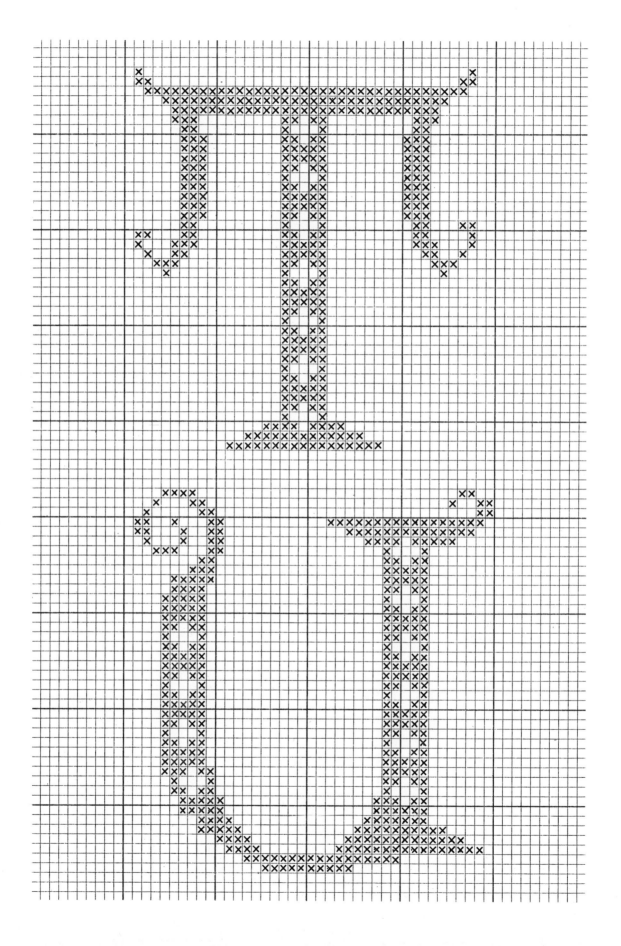

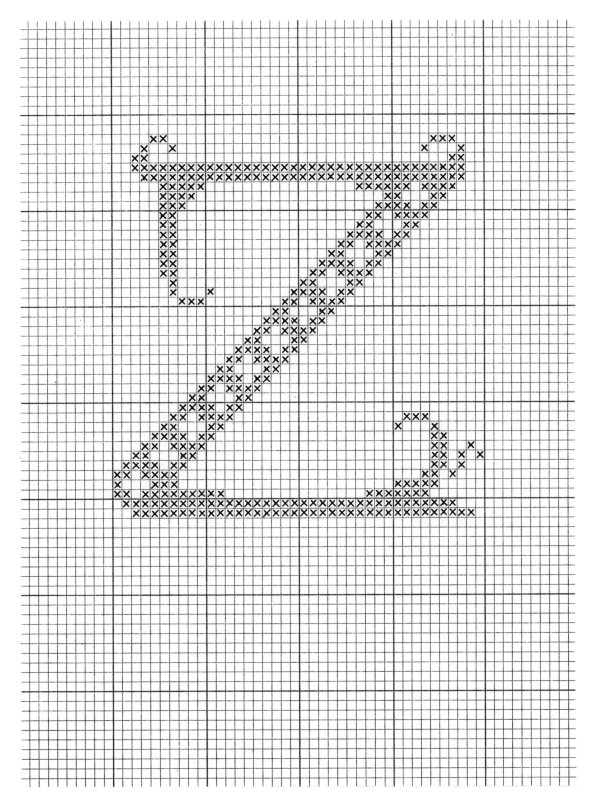

83

29-31

Three variations of five-square minimum numerals

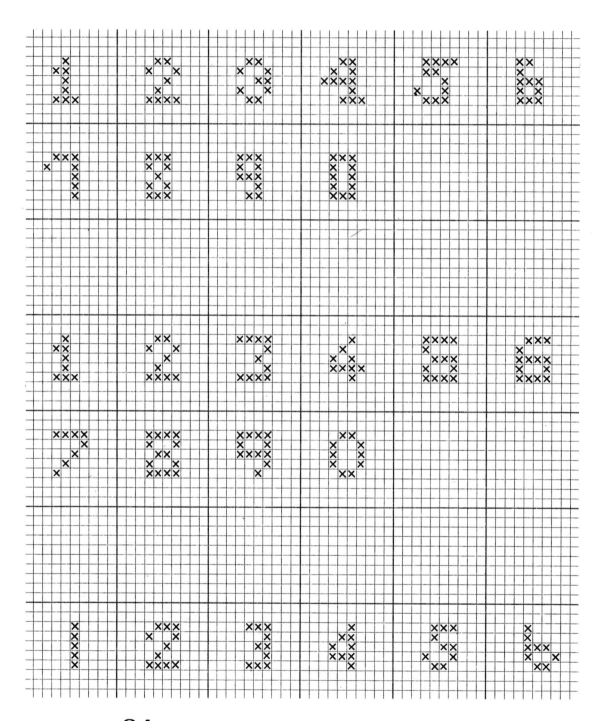

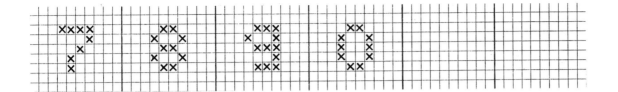

32 Five-square italics, two ascenders and descenders

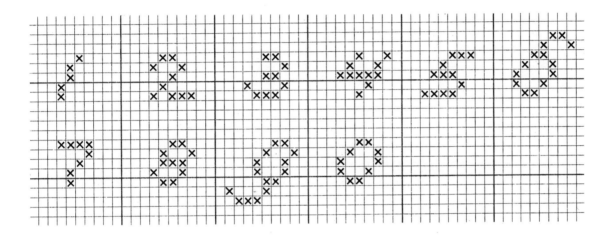

33 Six-square numerals

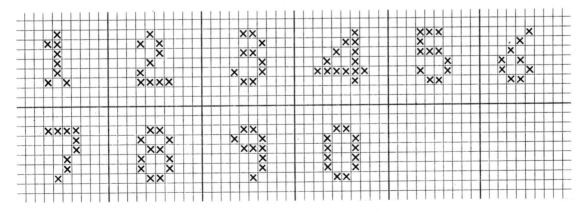

34 Seven-square numerals

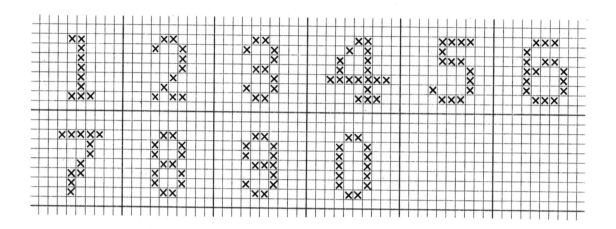

35 Nine-square numerals

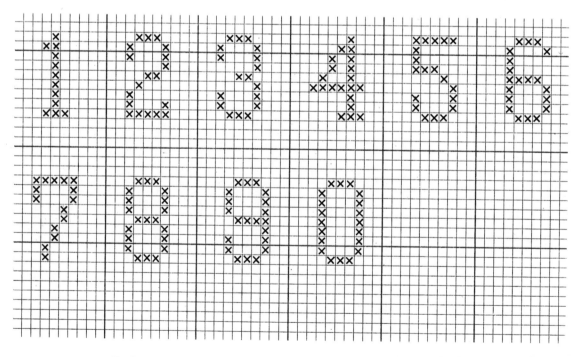

36 Ten-square numerals

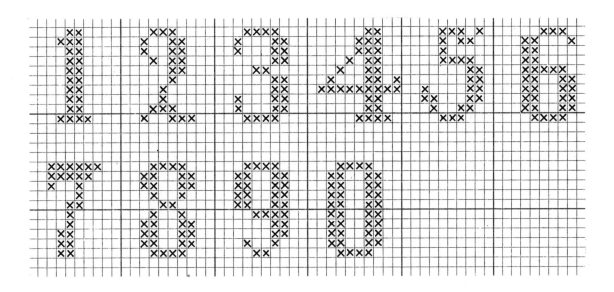

37 Eleven-square numerals

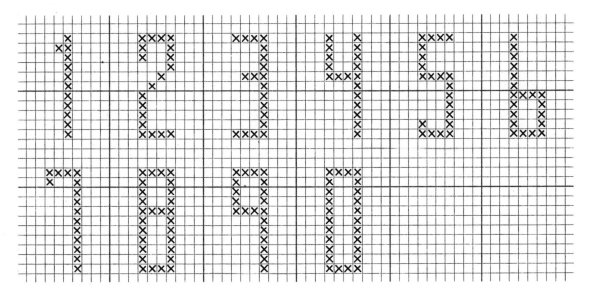

38 Eleven-square numerals

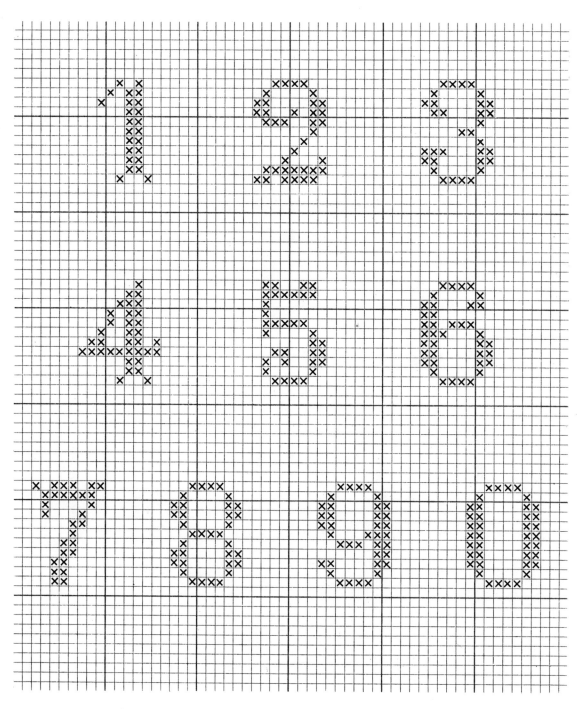

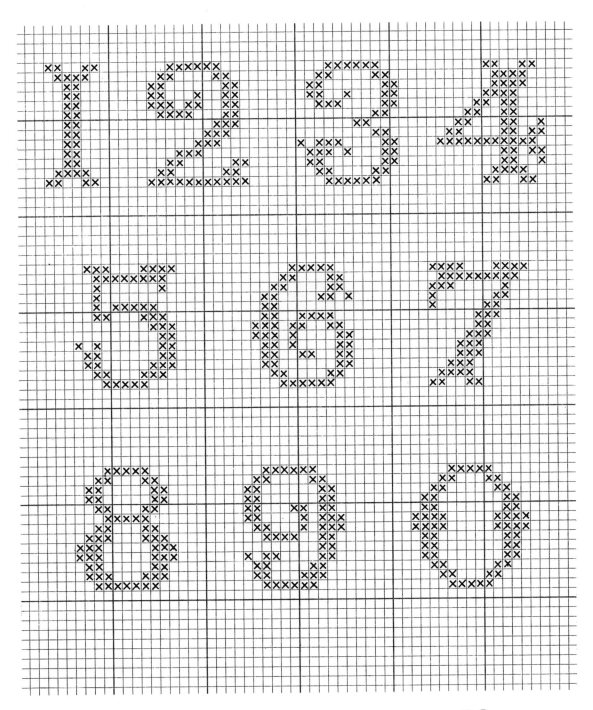

40 Six-square roman numerals

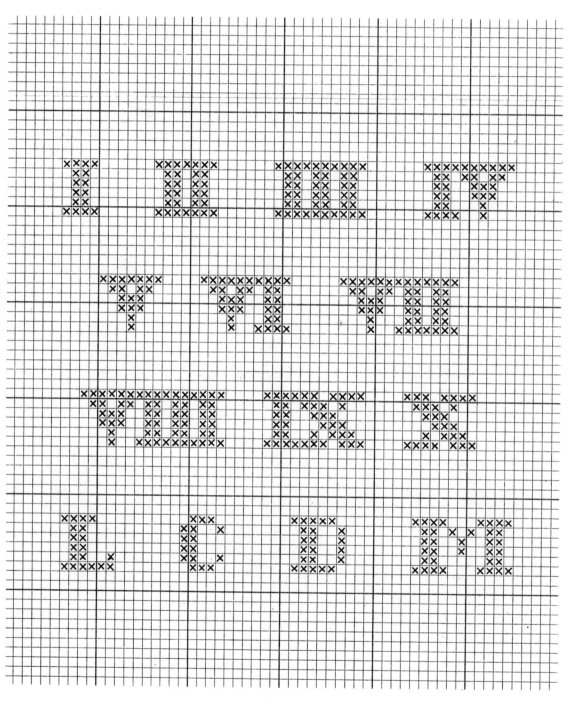

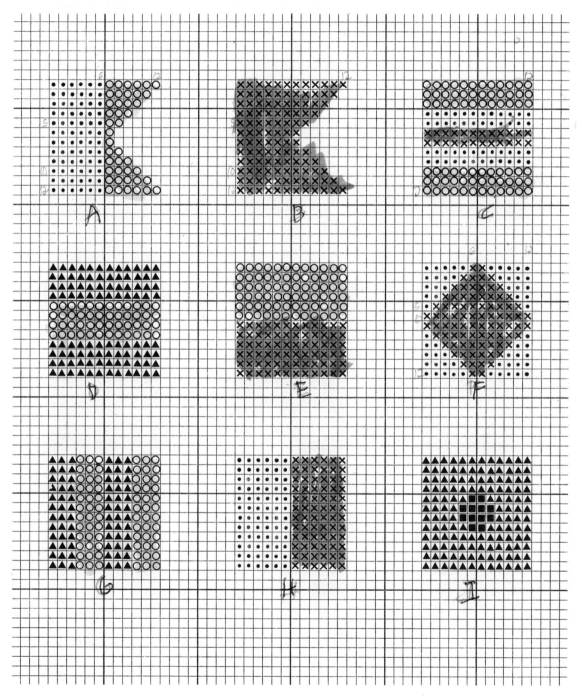

X Red
o Blue
▲ Yellow
. White
▨ Black

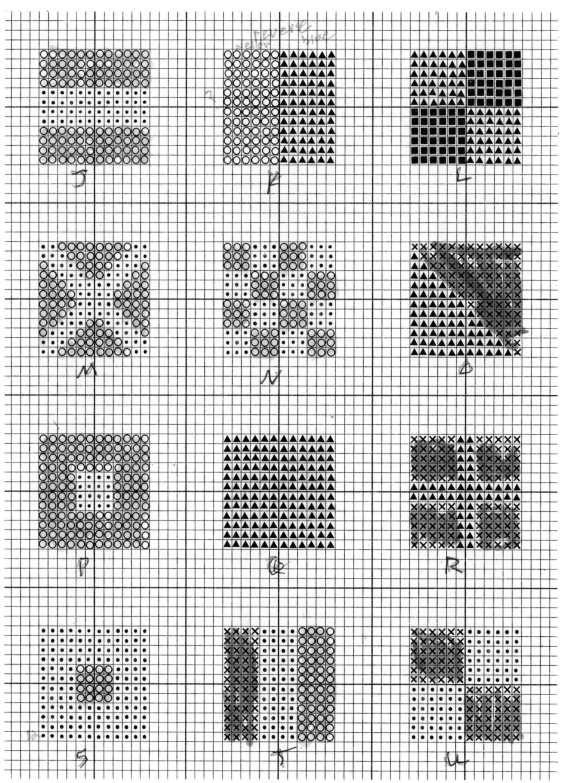

92

X Red
o Blue
▲ Yellow
. White
■ Black

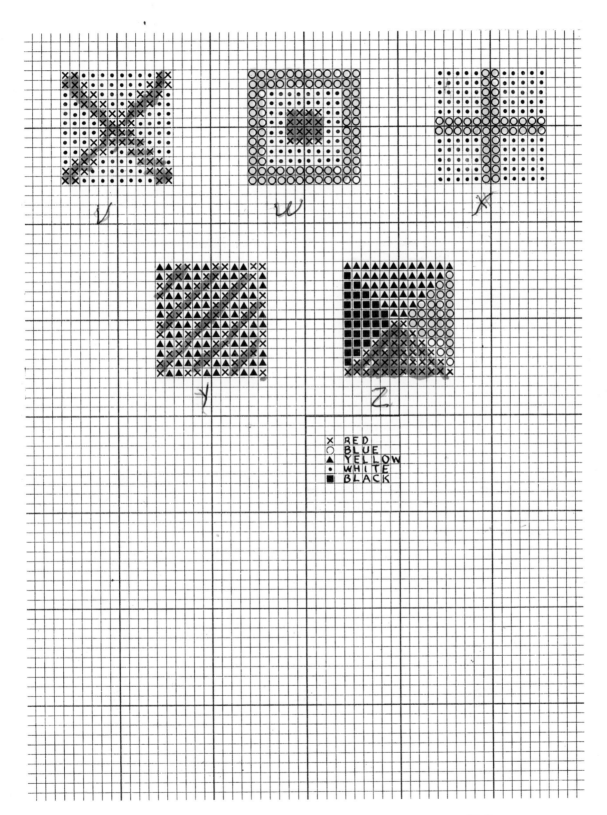

V W X

Y Z

× RED
○ BLUE
▲ YELLOW
• WHITE
■ BLACK

93

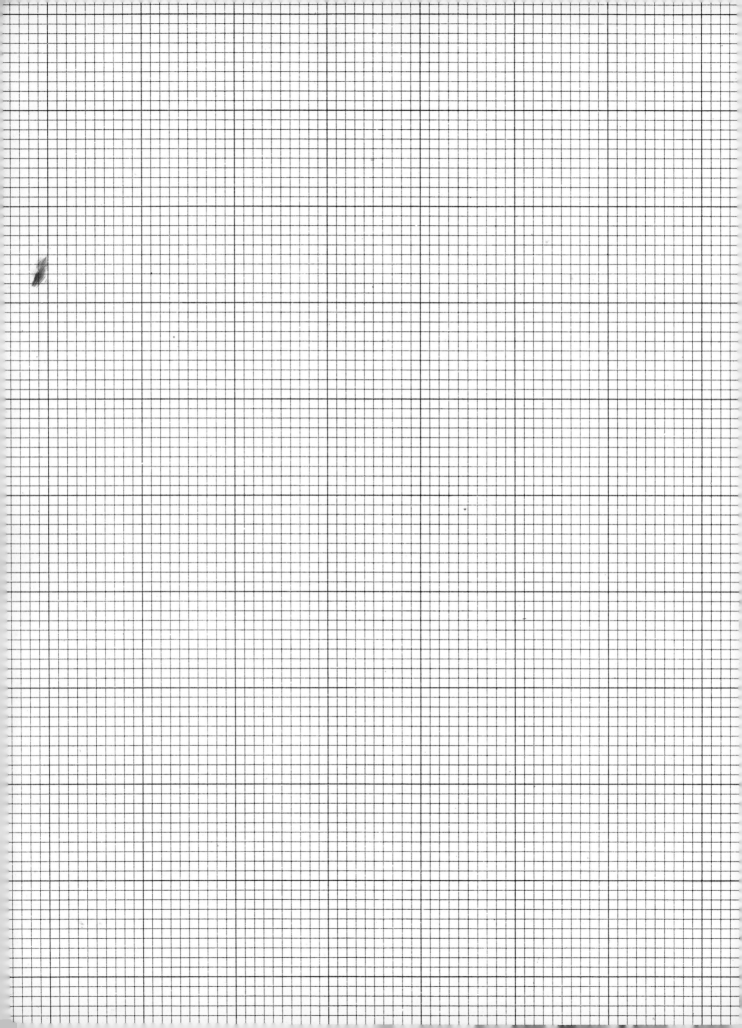